*The Keyboard Music
of C. P. E. Bach*

UNIDENTIFIED MANUSCRIPT
Library of the Paris Conservatoire. MS 1562

PHILIP BARFORD

THE
KEYBOARD MUSIC
OF C. P. E. BACH

considered in relation to
his musical aesthetic
and the rise of the
sonata principle

Barrie and Rockliff
London

© 1965 by Philip Barford

First published 1965 by
Barrie & Rockliff (Barrie Books Ltd)
2 Clement's Inn, London, WC2
Printed in Great Britain by
W. & J. Mackay & Co Ltd
Fair Row, Chatham, Kent

To
my dear wife
Gwynneth Elizabeth

Everyone calculates, everyone broods over harmony – well and good! I readily admit that we can never sufficiently thank a Bach, a Marpurg, a Kirnberger for their supremely instructive writings. But one ought also to attend to the chief and final aim of music; one ought also to investigate its melody, its expression, and above all its effect.

Johann Friedrich Reichardt *Briefe eines aufmerksamen Reisenden*, 1774

Quoted from Oliver Strunk: *Source Readings in Music History*

Contents

Foreword

THE main aim of this book is to encourage thoughtful performers of keyboard music to play the compositions of Emanuel Bach. This, I believe, requires imaginative and sympathetic penetration of his musical attitudes, and reflection upon the fascinating world of sound to which he opened the door. I have especially in view the kind of musician to whom notes are the beginning of musical experience and not the end. It is especially true of the music of this deeply reflective composer that the first movement of the hands on the keys is the first step in a richly rewarding adventure of the tonal imagination.

I have presented Emanuel's keyboard music in a theoretical context. This may well reflect my own inclination towards a metaphysical appraisal of musical experience; but in justification I should like to point out that the composer himself was an enthusiastic theorist, that the art of music was undergoing the most interesting transformations in his day, and that these need thinking about in some depth. Moreover, aesthetic speculation was a notable contemporary development in German culture, and it certainly left its mark upon the history of eighteenth-century music. Not least, the very basis of human experience was being rigorously examined. Immanuel Kant (1724–1804) was a famous contemporary of C. P. E. Bach. He made his own contribution to aesthetics in the *Critique of Judgment*, and the general trend of his thought invited, and perhaps made inevitable, Hegel's attempt to interpret the entire scheme of things as the introspection of an Absolute, all-permeating spirit. Then again, the art of music was influenced by the literary movement associated with the concept of *Sturm und Drang*; and Lessing himself was a friend of Emanuel Bach.

Confronted with the amazing variety of Emanuel's keyboard music, and reflecting upon the aesthetic principles upheld by the composer, which lay great stress upon the expressive value and nature of music, it seemed unreasonable to discuss his work as if the literary and philosophical background did not exist.

Accordingly, I have tentatively related the growth of the sonata-principle (which I interpret at an altogether deeper psychological level than the more familiar conception of sonata-form) to the emergence of a metaphysical attitude which seems particularly congenial to the German mind. This is that the inner world of feelings, emotions, ideas and spiritual aspirations, bound up with and expressing itself in the outer world of forms and structures, invites a comprehensive synthesis – even of apparently unrelated factors – in a dynamic whole.

English readers usually take the term 'comprehend' to mean 'understand' or 'include'. In German thought of the Hegelian era the comprehension of a relationship between two opposed or complementary factors means more than just the understanding of that relationship. It seems to imply that the mind, in comprehending, relates and binds together different things in its field of perceptions by a positive, *creative* force which establishes a new order of objective reality and significance. Such comprehension of a multiplicity of things is then idealized as a cosmic process. I believe S. T. Coleridge was deeply influenced by this way of considering experience when he formulated his theory of the imagination as the creative energy of the true poet and artist.

The richness of Emanuel Bach's musical imagination invites consideration of his work in relation to the ideas which reached a definitive expression in German philosophy shortly after his death. At the intellectual level, this suggests a loose analogy between the sonata-principle, which binds different tonal elements together, and the Hegelian idea of unity in difference. At the subconscious level, prior to either tonal or conceptual expression, the common ground between the musical principle and the metaphysical idea seems vastly more significant.

Speaking personally, the variety, the pungency, the richness of life and the problems raised by the analysis of musical experience point to some kind of idealistic theory of art. Living experience of the relation between mind, hands and keyboard in the performance of music aiming deliberately at the communication of feeling and emotion raises vital issues concerning the nature and significance of musical experience. These same issues are raised by the music of Emanuel Bach, whose keyboard music presupposes an ideal relationship between performer and instrument, emotion and tonal structure, idea and form.

I remember a lecturer in the philosophy of science who once confessed to me, despite long experience of the hard-headed world of industrial science, and a tendency to be sceptical about almost everything, that he could not formulate a satisfactory theory of art which did not seem to imply an idealist theory of knowledge. He was franker than most. Enemies of idealism often prefer to leave art alone. Either that or they denigrate it to the level of refined entertainment from which every possible ideal implication has been ruthlessly stripped away. The point is that in music, which has no spatial existence, the mind seems to participate the object it contemplates. How can music express emotion if there is no performer to project his own emotions into the creative act, and no listener to identify himself with them? How, indeed, does music exist at all? This question is particularly pertinent to the music of Emanuel Bach whose guiding principle is that music cannot move others unless the performer himself is moved. Some principle of inner resonance and sympathy seems to be involved which binds composer, performer and listener together as one mind in the music. Aristotle reflected that the movement of tones seems to be the movement of mind and heart in the person listening. Imaginatively, one moves on to the notion of an ideal medium, in which all minds cohere, and which is given order and significance by the structures of music. Such a notion is as old as civilization. I confess that it has a hold upon my mind, and it has led to some deeply illuminating experiences.

Are we intended to make this imaginative leap? The artist, said Coleridge, may possibly assist Nature in the direction of her own striving. In other words, what Nature offers to us in separateness and differentiation – whether the matter be images, words or feelings and emotions – the poet, the painter and the musician can fuse together in a new whole, a new vision. Is this fused vision, this new unity of experience wrested from Nature a new truth about things? Whatever the truth about the universe, it is a universe which, in some sense, contains those unified views of itself which are born in the mind of the artist.

Above all, it is a universe which contains the clavichord sonatas of Emanuel Bach, and the reader who is content with the music alone will find that there are enough notes in these pages to engage his attention on purely musical grounds. The final appeal is to musical experience, and the ideas forwarded in the following pages are intended to be a stimulus to the sort of performance of which Emanuel Bach himself would approve – a performance subjectively vital in every note. Away with the notion that music cannot express emotion, and that it is not music's business to make the attempt! We are in the presence of a composer to whom feeling and emotion are the very life-blood of music.

In an appendix I put forward some practical suggestions bearing upon the relationship between mental attitude and performance, and I feel that Emanuel Bach has still much to offer the twentieth century here. He believed in the subjective dynamic of musical experience. He believed technique to be the servant of experience. He gave practical instruction in the art of improvisation, and improvisation is a conscious demand upon the resources of the soul. He underlined the relation between technical aspects of performance and refinements of musical feeling. He grasped the connection between style and idea, and understood the art of composition down to its roots. He was, in short, the type of integral, reflective musician from whom the student of music has everything to learn. To take up the study of Emanuel Bach is to discover anew the vital pulse of music and to see a deep connection between mind, hands and keyboard. Here I speak with conviction because I have gained much from his music and his precepts. I should like to see Emanuel's teaching on Improvisation, for example, made a compulsory study in all schools where music is taught. It would help many a frustrated O-level student to preserve the lifeline intact between intellectual theory and sincerity of feeling and emotion, and this at a stage of development when music can play such an important part in the emotional life.

Apart from my debt to the composer himself, some acknowledgments are necessary. Interest in ideas which illuminate the underlying unity of human experience is growing and deepening in our own day. Any reader who is sympathetic to the critical position taken up in Chapter two will find further food for thought in Owen Barfield's book *Saving the Appearances* which deals with the idea of subjective participation in a very rewarding way. I do not claim that my own views are identical with his; but we have discussed these matters, and are very much on the same wavelength.

Paz Corazon G. Canave's book *A revaluation of the role played by C. P. E. Bach in the development of the clavier sonata* contains valuable material supplementary to Wotquenne's system of numbering, and in Chapter three I have relied upon this. I have also found Karl Geiringer's humane and scholarly book *The Bach Family* a source of inspiration and information. No student of C. P. E. Bach could do without William Mitchell's translation of the *Essay on the true art of playing keyboard instruments*, and I have frequently quoted from it. Other excellent studies of C. P. E. Bach to which I owe a debt are listed in the bibliography.

My thanks are also due to the publishers for generosity in the matter of musical examples, to John M. Thomson and his secretary; Hilary Corby, for all the work they put in on them, and again to John M. Thomson for many helpful suggestions. I am grateful to Kenneth Dommet for supplying a discography, and to Patricia Gill for typing the original manuscript.

The library of the Paris Conservatoire gave me permission to reproduce the unidentified manuscript which is lodged there. Chapter six draws upon some material previously published in *Music Review*. I am indebted to Fraülein Adelhaid Flach for checking the proofs.

In conclusion, two personal acknowledgements; I owe much to Gerald Abraham for friendly advice and encouragement during our pleasant association in Liverpool. And I remember with particular pleasure the warm companionship of my wife during hours spent in libraries copying out music, especially fugues.

Grateful acknowledgement is made to the publishers of modern editions of C. P. E. Bach's keyboard music where these have been used for quotation; especially to Schott & Co. Ltd., London.

PHILIP BARFORD

Liverpool 1965

Chapter one

Carl Philipp Emanuel Bach 1714–1788

CARL Philipp Emanuel Bach was born at Weimar on 8th March, 1714. He was the second son of Johann Sebastian Bach and Maria Barbara Bach. Like his two famous brothers, Wilhelm Friedmann and Johann Christian, Emanuel learned the art of music from his father, and he was a skilled clavier player before he reached the age of twenty. However, his education was not restricted to music, and it is possible that a latent business acumen and love of precise statement were developed by the course of law which he pursued for three years at Leipzig, and subsequently continued at Frankfurt-on-the-Oder. It is always an advantage for a musician to develop talents and abilities in other than purely musical subjects – a fact traditionally recognized in Germany. In this particular case, few would deny that Bach profited considerably from his early training. He lived at a time when composers could not be too wary where their commercial interests were concerned. More significantly, perhaps, Emanuel's university background was later to open the door to a stimulating circle of literary and academic acquaintances outside the somewhat restricted social sphere in which eighteenth-century musicians usually had to move. In his short autobiography, originally written for the German edition of Dr Burney's *The Present State of Music in Germany*[1] Bach recounts his musical activities in Frankfurt, which evidently included conducting, composition and the teaching of keyboard performance.

In the year 1738 Emanuel decided to make Berlin the centre of his activities as a professional musician. Almost as soon as he arrived there, however, the Crown Prince Frederick called him to Rheinsberg. In Bach's day a musician could be summoned to the royal court and held there at the royal pleasure. It would not be an easy matter for him to resign his post – as both Handel and Haydn discovered, and as Bach himself realized when he moved on to Hamburg twenty-eight years later. On the other hand, royal patronage could not be lightly regarded in the absence of a regular fixed income. The Crown Prince became King Frederick of

Prussia in 1740, and the first years of his reign were distinguished by artistic and musical ventures with which the king was to be associated for the rest of his life. These included the Berlin opera house, and castles at Charlottenburg and Potsdam. The residence at Potsdam rejoiced in the name of *Sans Souci*. This was where the king enjoyed most of his musical activities and where Emanuel laboured at the harpsichord as court accompanist. Here he was one of a large group of musicians summoned five times a week to provide royal concerts at which the king frequently played flute concertos composed by his former tutor at Rheinsberg, Johann Joachim Quantz. Emanuel's task as court accompanist was mainly to contribute a continuo to the ensemble. His long experience of this exacting art stood him in good stead when he wrote the detailed analysis of thoroughbass in the monumental *Versuch über die wahre Art das Clavier zu spielen* ('Essay on the True Art of Playing Keyboard Instruments'), published during his long stay at the Prussian court. His regular duties did not, so far as is known, include playing to the king on the clavichord, which he vastly preferred above all other keyboard instruments.

Bach's colleagues included Johann Gottlieb Graun and his brother Karl Heinrich Graun. This talented pair enjoyed a dominating position at court surpassed only by the favoured Quantz. Gottlieb conducted the King's orchestra, and Heinrich directed the Berlin opera for which he composed many works. Mention should also be made of Georg and Frantisek Benda, whose compositions sometimes reveal the influence of C. P. E. Bach's clavichord style.

Emanuel earned much less than Quantz and the Grauns, and it appears that he did not follow them in adjusting his temperament and musical attitudes to the royal whim. From his father he inherited a powerful sense of his own artistic integrity, a strong sense of money values and a streak of obstinacy – all admirable qualities in a composer determined to explore new and revolutionary trends in theory and composition. On at least one occasion, he was heard to mutter a caustic criticism of the king's fluctuating tempi. In music, and doubtless in all other matters, he did not suffer fools gladly. There were probably similar occasions which provoked royal displeasure. At any rate, Frederick, whose strongly conservative temper was opposed to the advanced tendencies in Emanuel Bach's music, responded as authority always does respond when it has to deal with rebellious subjects who do not practise the proper observances: he kept his accompanist's salary at a considerably lower level than that of his other favourites, Quantz and the Grauns. On one occasion, Emanuel suffered the affront of seeing his own former pupil, Nichelmann, appointed to the court orchestra at twice the salary he received himself. This was after fourteen years in Frederick's service.

The famous *Essay on the True Art of Playing Keyboard Instruments* shows that Emanuel was capable of rising above the somewhat petty environment of court music-making to the contemplation of principles. It also testifies to the stimulating intellectual climate of Berlin half-way through the eighteenth century when Kirnberger, Agricola, Marpurg, Quantz and others all contributed treatises on performance and musical aesthetic. These show the marriage of practical skills and thorough musicianship with speculative and theoretical interests – a dual approach to the art of music which is perhaps more characteristic of the German mind than of any other European nation.[2] This stage of German musical history was a most fruitful one precisely because music was open to potent influences in literary, artistic and even philosophical spheres. Lessing was a key figure in German literature, and a personal friend of Emanuel Bach. Almost certainly Bach met Moses Mendelssohn (the composer's grandfather), a distinguished literary philosopher remembered for a famous correspondence with Lessing. This ferment of intellectual and aesthetic activity was fostered in the 'Monday Club' where Emanuel was a frequent visitor; but it was at Bach's own house where his circle of friends met the real musician, the deeply introspective and adventurous clavichordist hidden beneath the professional exterior of court *continuo* player.

Emanuel's greatest love was for the clavichord. It is quite obvious, from reports by Reichardt and others, that he came into his own on this instrument. Like his elder brother, Friedmann, he had apparently inexhaustible gifts in improvisation. Friedmann seems to have been a romantic, even visionary character. Judging by his extraordinarily interesting and beautiful keyboard fugues, polonaises and sonatas, he lived – musically at any rate – in a Neptunian world of dreamy inspiration. This world was not unknown to Emanuel Bach who often goes farther still in plangent lyricism and romantic modulation; but the latter's style is generally more balanced by a matter-of-fact, intellectual candour than that of Friedmann. As a composer and theorist, Emanuel has his feet firmly on the ground. One senses the solid, German musicianship, the self-discipline, the obvious love of intellectual precision.

There is, in fact, something of a duality in Emanuel's character which is reflected both in his music and in the wider circumstances of his life. Cheerfully extrovert with his friends, he would enter into an intimate self-communion at the clavichord when playing to himself or to a favoured acquaintance. And the composer of romantic clavichord sonatas could also produce routine church music without his artistic conscience being too much troubled.

This duality served him in good stead both at Berlin, where he remained nearly thirty years, and at Hamburg where he succeeded Telemann in March 1768. In Potsdam it enabled him to accommodate himself to an often irksome professional situation. In Hamburg he was able to enter with much greater personal freedom into a wide-ranging cultural life. In his later years he could devote himself to the exploitation of his unique keyboard skill; and on the other hand he could preside competently over the manufacture and administration of liturgical music for the five Hamburg churches under his control.

Even in our own day, it is given to few professional musicians outside the universities to enjoy the best of two worlds as C. P. E. Bach appeared to do in Hamburg. As the musical director of a flourishing commercial town set in pleasant surroundings he earned enough to enable him to entertain lavishly and to indulge his connoisseurship. He welcomed many famous figures in his house at Hamburg, and assembled a sizeable collection of portraits, books and music, admired by Dr Burney who visited him there. There is a drawing of Emanuel Bach with the celebrated preacher Christian Sturm and the artist Andreas Stottrup which shows the three of them in an elegant apartment, possibly in Bach's home. Bach was on excellent terms with the university staff, and a large circle of literary figures which included the poets Klopstock and Heinrich Wilhelm von Gerstenberg. It was Gerstenberg who adapted Hamlet's famous soliloquy to the Fantasia in C minor which the composer included in the practice-pieces appended to the *Essay*. Gerstenberg also tried his hand at setting the last words of Socrates to the same work. Obviously it made a great impression upon him and indeed, it will continue to impress any keyboard-player who studies it. Gerstenberg's experiments are interesting in that they reveal the prevailing concern with the romantic and dramatic content of poetry and music – an interest further substantiated by Lessing's championship of the aesthetic of *Sturm und Drang*.

Although the cross-fertilization of musical and literary aesthetic is most clearly apparent in his clavichord music, Bach's larger vocal compositions, dating mainly from his Hamburg period, are by no means always merely derivative. It is true that he learned much from his father's liturgical style, and leaned heavily upon the baroque tradition of the cantata and passion music. This is evident from a perusal of the many liturgical compositions he adapted, arranged and composed for the Hamburg churches. His policy seems to have been to avoid composing original material if he could borrow or adapt his father's or Telemann's church music. It is easy to imagine that the tremendous demands placed upon a church musical director would force him to explore every source of supply. On occasion he arranged his own songs for orchestra and chorus. Yet there are some compositions where his creative genius is more apparent. Special mention should be made of the impressive German Sanctus for double chorus which appeared in 1779, and the cantata *Die Israeliten in der Wüste* published in 1775 and composed six years earlier.

Like many other composers of his day, Emanuel Bach was conditioned by social demands and circumstances. In his autobiography he hints that he would have liked to liberate himself more completely as a composer. Left to himself he would certainly have developed the progressive tendencies of his clavichord sonatas, fantasias and rondos, and possibly not have concerned himself overmuch with the traditional forms of chamber music and keyboard concerto. Bach was a virtuoso of expressive, declamatory performance, and not at all addicted to keyboard pyrotechnics. His music for chamber ensembles is not, in the round, exciting, and much of it is a sign of his willingness to supply music as required by social demand and not as a response to any compelling inspiration. The situation is somewhat different in the case of the symphonies, some of which, notably the set of six composed in 1773, reveal the same daring modulations, dramatic hesitations and rhythmic ingenuity which we find in the clavichord sonatas.[3]

Emanuel Bach matured as a composer during the middle eighteenth century when the tradition of baroque keyboard music was being overthrown by an emphasis upon single lines of melody and simple figures of accompaniment. He certainly learned much from his father, for whose music he always professed a great admiration, and whose fugues, according to Burney, he played with intensity and inspiration; but he also absorbed the influences of rococo and *stile galante*, and the dynamics of the Mannheim school, represented pre-eminently by Karl Stamitz. These factors alone do not by any means account for the highly individual slant of his creative genius, as it is manifested in his famous collections for clavichord. The aesthetic of *Empfindsamkeit* took a firm hold upon his musical imagination during his days at the Potsdam court, and this was further consolidated by *Sturm und Drang* as his friendship with poets and literary theorists ripened in a shared philosophical atmosphere at Hamburg. The ebb and flow of feeling, storm and stress, tension, the play of the passions, the communication of a heightened subjectivity – these are the factors which called forth his best work. And his best work is undoubtedly the music he composed for his favourite instrument.

C. P. E. Bach is a vitally important figure not only in the history of keyboard music, but also in the sphere of musical aesthetic. He reflected deeply and continuously about the principles of his art, and set his thoughts down in writing. They invite – in fact they demand serious consideration in the light of the profound metaphysical tendencies which came to the fore in German thought during the later years of the eighteenth century.

In general, two streams of musical development can be clearly distinguished at this time. This distinction is of course theoretical, and requires many qualifications. One is the line of development which runs through

Johann Christian Bach and Mozart; the other is the line running through Emanuel Bach and Haydn. Beethoven's music brings the two streams to a synthesis. Mozart was well aware of Emanuel's music; but his own is characterized by a rhythmic poise which is not a distinctive feature in the sonatas and symphonies of the earlier master. Emanuel, precisely because he has embraced the aesthetic of *Empfindsamkeit* wholeheartedly, constantly disrupts the rhythmic phraseology, introducing sforzandos, hesitations, and sudden pianissimos in a manner anticipating Haydn's keyboard sonatas, and Beethoven's music generally. It was Haydn, not Mozart, who spent long rhapsodic hours with the clavichord pieces of Emanuel Bach, and in some works he imitates Emanuel's style so closely that his debt requires no other demonstration than a performance.

By considering Emanuel Bach in the broader context of eighteenth-century culture, my aim will be to reveal what is enduring in his work, not merely to exhibit it as one factor in a complex situation.

Chapter two

Critical approach to the subject

'MUSIC,' said Beethoven, 'is the closest link between the spiritual and the sensuous.' Without implying quite such an extreme position, a modern critic has stated that the art of music has two polarities: sensuous beauty and intellectual abstraction, and that most music can be placed somewhere on the gamut between the two.[1] Both statements imply a possible ideal relationship between the matter of music – tonal sensation, and the form – intellectual content, or even spiritual apprehension. If there is such an ideal relationship, then music which fails to express it, which fails to achieve the perfect unifying synthesis of intellectual abstraction and tonal sensation will inevitably veer to one polarity at the expense of the other. This would reserve the point of ideal balance for the very greatest musical minds.

The image is suggestive. It implies that there are composers to listen to and composers to think about, and a few who exalt the musical mind through its perfect embodiment in sensuous beauty. We might believe that it was given to Mozart to dignify musical art in this way. By comparison, Emanuel Bach, whose music frequently yields a rich, sensuous expressiveness, nevertheless appears to veer towards the polarity of intellectual abstraction. In other words, his work is a constant challenge to our deeper musical perceptions, a constant stimulus to aesthetic speculation, a thought-provoking example of the way conscious reflection can significantly affect the course of musical history.

The idea of polarity suggests something of the true nature of musical evolution – not from dark mediaeval beginnings to the electronic wonders of Stockhausen, but the mental and spiritual unfolding of the musical consciousness from its initial preoccupation with the medium of sound alone to the ordering of that medium in significant patterns of varying complexity in accordance with intellectual lucidity and fructifying inspiration.

Any real appreciation of Emanuel Bach's keyboard music requires an intense effort of imaginative penetration and intellectual sympathy. In his work, the functions of musical intellect are closely associated with self-generated emotional impulsions. The expression of feeling and emotion is a marked feature of his music because intellect has prejudged them, and decided it is good that they should be there. Again, Bach was one of those composers (and I am convinced that many greater composers have been more like this than we generally suppose) who could be musically inspired by an intellectual idea about music, even to the extent of composing from an essentially non-tonal image – as, for example, an interesting notational configuration or the actual feel of a particular manipulative pattern on the keyboard.[2] There can be no doubt that the psychological atmosphere of his best clavichord music is partly the result of considerable reflection about musical functions and processes. The subjective *Affekt* is frequently silhouetted against the backcloth of a calm and thoughtful mind.

The really great genius brings to a synthesis the two opposite poles of sound and intellect – or, to generalize the relationship, of matter and mind. From whatever stand-point we survey his work, we are impressed by the drive towards integration and coherence. This, of course, is the type of the ideal Hegelian synthesis, wherein a dual reciprocity is justified by unity on a higher plane. The third term, the synthetic moment of consciousness, is the wholeness of the thing, from which matter and mind or, as in music, sound and thought, are only abstractions.[3]

One wonders at the historical fact that in so many cases genius flowers on a prepared soil. The process of preparation seems to be a focussing of the two polarities, an unconscious preadjustment of terms which invites the moment of synthetic insight. There are few more remarkable events in the history of music than the emergence of the Viennese group at the latter end of the eighteenth century. C. P. E. Bach appears to stand in a significant relation to it. We can study, in his keyboard music, that process of preadjustment and focussing.

An important warning has to be uttered at once. I would never maintain that conscious aesthetic speculation always underlies a period marked by distinctive characteristics, or that the emergence and eventual unification of separate, distinct or even divergent factors takes place on the surface of consciousness, or that the idea of such a process is recognized as a theoretic and inspirational *milieu* by those who are actively engaged. It is only when a period comes into historical perspective, when the main characters are dead, when the first critical books have been written, and superseded by the fruits of more mature scholarship, that what was unconsciously or consciously sought after, and what was achieved – either in spite of or because of all the striving – can be comprehended, and the separate strands in the complex skein of musical history identified and labelled. Presumably this process of discovery will never really stop. There is generally a limit beyond which the recovery of material evidence is impossible; but even on the basis of what we have, there is no foreseeable limit to the possibilities of future insight and interpretation until, presumably, that final point of *éclaircissement* in the history of the world consciousness is reached which Teilhard de Chardin has called 'the omega point'.[4] Significances change and deepen, and there is need for a constant historical watchfulness, a readiness to reappraise and re-think the whole of a complex phenomenon in order to discover its interior drive, its possible teleological principle. This book will involve such a reappraisal.

Looking back into the musical history of the eighteenth century, we see the profusion, the welter, the mass of speculation, the busy manufacture of ephemeral and more enduring works. We cannot say, except glibly, that this period 'showed how composers established the sonata-form' without giving a false and subtle twist to our historical appraisal. If we do say it, then we immediately suggest that everything was much more clear-cut, much simpler, much more neatly tied than it could possibly have been. We have the class-room picture of one or two periwigged composers sitting at their music-desks and harpsichords dreaming up sonata-form, and providing the vehicle which Haydn and Mozart and Beethoven were (at first gracefully, and later cavalierly) to use.

As a healthy corrective it is useful to see how far we can go in the other direction, by supposing that composers simply wrote as they pleased with no more than a half-conscious acknowledgement of some prevailing fashion. Perhaps Emanuel Bach never had the remotest idea that he would some day be hailed as a great innovator, the inventor or 'father' of sonata-form, a 'key-figure' ushering in a new art of tonal thinking. Still, he certainly was aware of the most progressive trends of his day and he did much to further them. The truth is too subtle to be captured by a neat formulation. Neat formulations are the bane of history. And yet we must ask: What unconscious force or agency was really at work in the eighteenth century during the era of focussing and preadjustment? How is it that we are able to speak of the emergence of a particular compositional principle, and illustrate it with many telling examples? We assert the presence of a universal form of musical thought. What is the real nature of such universals? Are they unconsciously operative in a composer's mind even before he has formed a clear idea of them?

Facile answers to questions of this type are most characteristic of the sociological approach to musical history, in which there is a tendency to explain musical forms and styles by reference to prevailing modes and manners, specific strata of society, special intellectual or religious influences. But all these, together with music itself, are alike manifestations of human consciousness at a particular time, and demand a deeper reason in themselves. They may mutually illuminate music and one another; but music is far more than a mere ancilla to social movement.

Some of the most interesting aspects of a wave of musical development are contained in its first phase, the phase of amorphous beginnings, of restlessness and rejection, of mounting discontent with existing forms and styles. Later there is a period of *rationale*, when the focussing and pre-adjustment take place, the discussion and the theorizing. Finally there appear the greater masters, and in the light of whom the amorphous beginnings and the speculation take on hue and significance. It is important to remember that if it were not for the climactic phases of musical history, the earlier phases might very well go unlabelled, and the theorizings might seem vain. Rightly or wrongly, there seems to be some compulsion at work in the mind to see history as somehow teleological, driving onwards, perhaps in fits and starts, to ends unknown and only dimly foreshadowed. Nowadays we can often see striking resemblances between a moment in a sonata by Emanuel Bach and a moment in a Beethoven sonata. Both were originally moments in historical time; but in virtue of our historical imagination we can now abstract them from historical time, relate them in our own consciousness, and in doing this give them a new status in the life of that consciousness. Now they become elements in a pattern of historical and aesthetic comprehension, parts of a whole the precise nature of which is determined by the unique nature of our individual being. In comprehending we relate, and in relating we comprehend. But who, in Bach's day, could possibly have pointed to any element in a Bach sonata which would perhaps stimulate or inspire a greater master to emulation or enhanced presentation of something essentially the same? Moreover, in the lifetime of either Bach or Beethoven, who could foretell the nature of that future consciousness which would compare and relate the two, and arrive at insights and conclusions remote from the minds of these composers?

So our three phases are abstract intellectual conceptions retrospectively arrived at in the light of a number of compositions which seem to vindicate much that has gone before. It is true, to a certain extent, that life has a habit of crystallizing itself – in the retrospective consciousness – in three phases which come to seem more significant the more we meditate upon them. It is pertinent at this point to remember the raptures of Jean de Muris upon the divine universality of the number three.[5]

But we must be careful. The history of musical consciousness is most rewarding when it is married to some attempt to understand the inchoate aesthetic striving, and this kind of history is very much more difficult to write. That which exists 'on the surface' so to speak, for our detached aesthetic appraisal, for analysis during the academic lecture, is only the manifest form of an organic restlessness in the depths of the unconscious mind – or soul, to give it its old-fashioned name. And since it appears now that individual distinctions shade off into a reservoir of universality in this deep and mysterious region, and even that distinctions of time appear to have no validity there,[6] then there is a very real possibility that the historical account of a musical period may well be a description of something essential to our own present minds as much as it was essential to the minds of those who were once consciously engaged. To put it another way, the history of a man's compositions is a form given to the history of his mind. The history of his consciousness invites an examination of universal currents in the depths of his being. And as soon as we make contact with these, and attempt to define them, we are, paradoxically, looking into our own nature as well.[7]

The music of Emanuel Bach is fascinating for a number of reasons, and not least, as we shall see, because it seems to catch the reflection of a universal psychological truth, the proper understanding of which does indeed give us a key to many other matters pertinent not only to the history of music, but to the history of human culture in general. The word which underlines the very basis of history is the word consciousness. The history of art cannot be restricted to the history of tangible forms and events. History must always be the history of consciousness. It is consciousness which fashions a work of art. It is in consciousness that it is known and loved. It is consciousness which strives to contain it. And for every moment of consciousness there is an unconscious correlative – a deep origin in the psyche, perhaps too a lasting consequence, a profound impact which, at a later time, will emerge transfigured in some new guise, with much theory to justify a 'new approach'. To take a specific example, it often seems that the instrumental music of Emanuel Bach, with its self-dramatization, its posturings, its sighs and soliloquies, is the re-emergence, in terms of instrumental tone, of the same basic impetus which found expression in the operatic experiments of the Florentines. The original drive or *nisus* of opera, after Monteverde, was frequently lost, pushed down into the unconscious, as audiences, and composers (who soon caught on to the knack of mass-producing the kind of things which satisfied them) preoccupied themselves with melody at the expense of drama. Yet the fructifying idea was never wholly lost sight of. Ultimately, it re-emerged with considerable force, and captured imaginative clavier players by storm. And because the dramatic urge to self-expression is true to something in human nature, one is tempted to surmise that it will emerge yet again, and perhaps even usher in another welter of romanticism – a romanticism enriched with all the technical resource which is being formulated in our own time.

The word consciousness, when applied to history, underlines the subjective aspect of every recorded outward event which has a shape, a form or a frame. Those specialized events which we call works of art are subjective before they are objective, mental before they are physical. For this reason, recorded events are one-sided unless they are regarded in connection with the subjective factors essential to them. The historian who ignores these subjective factors is only half a historian, like the so-called psychologist who bases his psychology only upon the observed physical constitution and behaviour of his subject, man, and not upon the thoughts and aspirations which characterize man's subjective world.

When we stand in front of the cathedral at Chartres we are confronted not merely by the mass of wrought stonework, but by the consciousness of which the building is an expression. It is possible to describe the physical features of the cathedral, to give an account of its building, to study the work-books of the masons, even to take account of their material aims and purposes. But how much more has come through than the material result of material labour! How can this possibly be if we do not acknowledge the fact that the outward striving in physical mass was but the overwhelming expression of a dynamic inwardness in the very souls of the builders? And what relation had this inwardness in the builders to the life of their time? Were their music, theology and philosophy all unrelated to one another – mere effusions with haphazard origins and no inter-connexions? Every fibre of one's being cries out that this was not so. It can be rigorously demonstrated that the geometrical figures consciously built into the great gothic cathedrals were, in their numerical basis, the very same as those musical proportions which resounded within those mighty edifices.[8] Again, these same considerations of number are vital to a thorough understanding of the very principles of reasoning which underlay the theology and philosophy of the time. Speculation of a Pythagorean type is at the root of much of it. Unfortunately, we seldom appreciate the deeper (and by modern standards esoteric) significance of this kind of thinking. We *ought* to be alerted by the wholeheartedness and intensity with which mediaeval theorists of Pythagorean stamp applied themselves to their monochords. What was the real drive behind all this apparently unrewarding labour? Could it be the deep conviction, slowly lost into the depths of the psyche as the Middle Ages advanced into the Renaissance and the Renaissance into modern times, that these numerical proportions enshrined in temporal art-forms were symbols not only of the nature of all perishable outward formations but of the innermost structure of subjective man as well? Is this the real reason why Chartres stirs the contemplative consciousness to its depths? Is like beckoning to like? Is the symbol awakening the very substance of what it symbolizes into a paroxysm of self-recognition?

It is axiomatic to any serious historian of music that when he studies a musical manuscript he is looking at a symbolic picture of tonal reality. Is it so axiomatic that this same tonal reality is itself a symbol of a non-tonal, subjective reality? It must be admitted that this non-sounding reality, this subjective inwardness of the object is a trap for the unwary, and a dreadful temptation to the partitive music critic. How easy it is to impose a subjective fantasy upon the tonal object, and say: 'This is what the composer really means.' When it is known that a certain composer had programmatic tendencies, the quagmire of subjectivity becomes all the more enticing. Is there any way in which we can safeguard the historical perspective, and yet admit the historical reality of the subjective aspect without violating the essential outwardness and purity of the object?

A work of art is a pattern.[9] Any significant discussion of that pattern must therefore involve analysis. A musical composition is a pattern of sounds. This pattern was born in the composer's consciousness. Its simplicity or complexity are directly correlative with that consciousness. It is, so to speak, a 'shape' given to consciousness. Once this shape has been arrived at the process or function of consciousness seeking tonal expression has reached a definitive stage. What was once a merely subjective impulse has now passed into objective manifestation, reflected itself into the outside world. Henceforth, this objective thing can stand on its own feet as a work of art.

What happens when this work of art is presented to a consciousness other than that of the composer? Immediately it beckons to the subjective world again – firstly to that of the performer, secondly to that of the listener, and it keeps on beckoning until it has re-established itself in the consciousness of each as a complete, self-fulfilled function or process of his own inwardness.

This inward retrenchment goes on during the whole process of getting to know a work. In the performer, the function of consciousness, complete and self-fulfilled has to be expressed in a physical pattern of kinetic response. Music only exists, and can only ever exist as a total psycho-physical complex, to which the consciousness of composer, performer and listener are contributary channels. What is born in subjectivity ultimately returns to the subjective. Its transmission from the subjective consciousness of the composer to that of the performer, and thence to the listener not only bestows upon it the highest degree of individualization, but also depends upon the universality of the objective realm of tone, and a universal sphere of mentalism wherein the reign of tonal laws is recognized and upheld by individual minds.

The physical side of the psycho-physical complex is the arrangement of heard sounds which are quite obviously the climactic points of the composer's subjective impulsions – as subsequently relived by performer and listener. Each note or chord is the bursting into objectivity of a subjective drive which, on 'either side' of the heard note, is non-tonal in essence but tonal in implication.[10] The process is analogous to the birth of a spark between positive and negative terminals. Indeed, the subjective consciousness could well be described as the positive polarity of musical creation. But it cannot do without its negative polarity of 'matter', since it is this realm of objectivity which finally justifies and completes the circuit of the aesthetic consciousness. The objective pattern is now the dwelling which the creative energy has formed for itself.

This brief description does not violate the intrinsic objectivity or outward 'thingness' of a work of tonal art. But we must realize that its 'thingness' is truly a complex of outer and inner, that it is only a work of art, an object, within a total, generalized field which is itself a psychophysical complex. If the principle of consciousness is abstracted from the innermost concept of musical history, there can be nothing which we can dignify by the term 'history'. In actual fact, we cannot really remove it, since the very nature of historical thinking presupposes it. To pretend it does not count is a species of intellectual dishonesty born of the refusal to tolerate or admit the view of human life and nature which is implied by recognizing it.[11]

Accepting the principle of consciousness in history, we can legitimately de-personalize the whole process of aesthetic creation and accept the idea that a particular work is a particle ultimately 'condensed' within a generalized subjective continuum which draws in upon itself repeatedly, intensifying as it shrinks until, within a particular local 'field', a unit of psycho-physical beingness which we call a composer, it generates sufficient intensity to make its *rapprochement* with the outer world, and blossoms into form. We might imagine that this process is really going on all the time. The difference between the artist and the non-creative man is that in the latter there exists a relative insensitivity to this universal pressure to create. His subjective vitality flows away from him in various forms of wayward activity, and he is never sufficiently highly 'charged' to feel the urge to create forms through conscious endeavour. The artist, on the contrary, is alive to this inward pressure. The creations of other men are a challenge to him; the cycle of the seasons with its endlessly changing series of visible forms and colours *demands* expression through the painter's consciousness, setting up a positive 'charge', a restlessness of the soul which enforces, again and again, its union with the objective material realm. The final creative act, the *rapprochement* with form, is the achieving of a state of equilibrium between the spirit and matter of his own being, and the result is an addition to the sum of created things, and perhaps also of human happiness.

This being so, the historical understanding and appraisal of a musical phenomenon of times past is no light and easy matter. Somehow or other we have to enter into the psycho-physical complex which the composer created and vitalized with his own subjective being. We have to make

contact with the wider, more tenuous arena which engaged his consciousness. We can only do this by a penetrative effort which exercises our
imagination to the utmost; but at the same time we have to consider the
symbolic patterns, the notes themselves, with great care and substantial
attention to detail. The first stage of this proceeding is concerned with
psychological and even spiritual insight – taking 'spiritual' here to indicate the subjective realm of forces which are creatively at work in the
aesthetic consciousness. The second stage is concerned with intellectual
analysis and discussion of tonal patterns. In this book, both phases will be
fused together, and we shall try to comprehend the realm of inner, subjective impulsions as well as the outward forms which express them.

It is sometimes insisted that 'comprehension' or 'understanding' have
nothing to do with musical appreciation and criticism. But this is nonsense – nonsense, moreover, grounded upon a purely hedonistic view of
musical experience, which urges that music is simply to be enjoyed. It is a
simple fact of human nature that enjoyment, if it is to be more than a
merely sensual indulgence in the bath of musical tone, must involve an
element of critical detachment. Detachment in turn involves judgement,
and judgement the comprehension of technical procedures and general
aesthetic principles. In the mature musical consciousness, appreciation
and understanding flow together in the higher penetrations of imaginative
insight. To eschew understanding is to step blindfold into the sphere of
musical thought, and to abdicate from the obligations of significant
criticism. In criticizing Emanuel Bach's music, we shall consider it as a
phenomenon to be comprehended.

There is an intrinsic quality in Bach's keyboard music which stands
apart from the music of later composers, despite the tendency of commentators to consider it mainly as an overture to the schools of Viennese
classicism. It is all too easy to allow appraisal of C. P. E. Bach to condense
into a few trite judgements. Profound study of his work reveals a unique
musical consciousness, a pioneering mind of considerable subtlety. The
complex of consciousness which was Emanuel Bach consisted of many
fine strands which are fascinating to unravel. In unravelling them we
shall be considering a region of musical history which, in terms of musical
principle, reveals much about the operations of the musical mind in
general. It is not going too far to state that his keyboard music is an
encyclopaedia of fundamental tonal procedures. It is thus a revelation
and justification of certain basic attitudes which are always the mark of
the true musician, in whom sound and intellect, theoretical understanding and technical accomplishment work together in harmony.

Chapter three

Classification of important keyboard music

C. P. E. BACH is remembered chiefly as a composer of sonatas for the clavi-chord. Of these, upwards of one hundred and fifty can be listed,[1] but it should be stated at once that this considerable output contains some un-remarkable music which does not require detailed consideration.

All the best sonatas have been republished recently, and it is no longer necessary to look far afield in order to uncover his most characteristic compositions in this genre. Fortunately, again, these best sonatas appeared at intervals throughout his creative life. This means that we can gain quite a clear picture of his overall development by paying close attention to his most interesting music. These periodic flowerings mark the peaks of phases of creative endeavour; it is enough to scan the troughs to realize that a great many sonatas are marked by a general sameness and routine mannerisms. We shall devote our main analytical energies to what is really worth remembering and preserving.

The farther back we unravel the history of the sonata the more sonatas we find in the output of composers who were attracted to the sonata-style – until we reach the period of amorphous beginnings which, in this case, goes back at least to Pasquini. Thus, the period around 1750 abounds in lightweight clavier sonatas, many of which appear to have been com-posed without undue pain.[2] One can enjoy some of the work of Emanuel Bach and his contemporaries without being impressed by any sublime heights of inspiration, any agony of soul. Sonata-composition seemed to be prolific before the term 'sonata' had acquired the aura which, in our own day, is still honoured. The significance of the designation increased as its main exponents applied it with growing respect. As the sonata-style un-folded, there is a generally diminishing output. Against the great quantity produced by Emanuel Bach, Beethoven composed thirty-eight (including the slighter works styled 'sonatina') and Liszt only two. This seems to be the result of two things – firstly an increasingly powerful focus of concen-tration upon the sonata-principle as such, and later a gradual waning of interest due to the emergence of other psychological factors seeking outlet in new styles and forms, or in old forms approached from a new standpoint. The more the sonata seemed to demand of a composer's spiritual energies, the fewer he wrote.

With such a notion in mind, it is easy to see that C. P. E. Bach's sonata-output is not characterized by a prolonged intensity, as in the case of Beethoven's sonatas, every one of which demands intrinsic consideration, but by an alternate tightening and slackening. The periods of intensification were marked by the following famous collections:

Die Preussischen Sonaten (The 'Prussian' Sonatas)

These were published by Schmid of Nürnberg in 1742 as 'Sei Sonate per Cembalo che all'Augusta Maestra di Frederico II, Re di Prussia', the composer's name appearing as Carlo Filippo Emanuele Bach. Despite this Italianate title, the sonatas were all composed in Germany during the year 1740. Wotquenne, who made a thematic catalogue of C. P. E. Bach's music at Brussels, where there is a large collection of his works, lists the group of six sonatas as 48/1–6. They are numbers 16–21 inclusive of Bach's complete sonata-output, so far as can be ascertained from the sources listing Emanuel's compositions,[3] although we should remember that the first eleven, composed during the years 1731–8, underwent some revision between 1741 and 1744. The 'Prussian' sonatas are now available in Nagels Musik-Archiv (6 and 15).

Die Württembergischen Sonaten (The 'Württemberg' Sonatas)

This is another group of six, dedicated to the Duke of Württemberg and published in 1744, also under an Italian title. The sonatas were composed during 1742–4, numbers 1, 2, 4 and 6 at Berlin, numbers 3 and 5 at Toplitz. Wotquenne numbers this group 49/1–6 and the chronological order is probably 23–28. The odd sonata, number 22, composed between the Prussian and Württemberg sets is Wotquenne 65/13, and it may be seen in Farrenc's Le Trésor des Pianistes, Volume 13, pages 490–7. Farrenc's collection is of inestimable value for lovers of Emanuel Bach's keyboard music as a readily available source of the many odd sonatas separately composed which appeared in early editions and collections such as Oeuvres Melées, Musikalisches Allerley, Musikalisches Mancherley, and Musikalisches Vierlerley, which appeared at Hamburg in 1770, edited by Bach himself. Most of the Bach sonatas published in Farrenc's collection are reprints from these early collections, and few have been published outside of it. The 'Württemberg' sonatas are now available in Nagels Musik-Archiv (21 and 22).

K.M.B.–C

Sechs Sonaten (zu einem *Versuch über die wahre Art das Clavier zu spielen*).

These are the famous *Probe-Stücke*, and although they were originally composed as demonstration pieces they contain music of a high order. They appeared in 1753 together with the *Versuch*, and constitute numbers 54–59 of the total collection (Wotquenne 63/1–6). Included in this group is the superb Fantasia in C minor, sometimes known as the 'Hamlet' Fantasia through Gerstenberg's adaptation of the soliloquy 'To be or not to be . . . ' to Bach's music. The sonatas and fantasia are published by Schott (2353–4).

Sechs Sonaten für Clavier mit veränderten Reprisen ('Sonatas with Altered Reprises')

Here again is a collection with an avowedly didactic aim. It was composed in 1759 and published the following year. The group comprises sonatas 75–80 of the total output (Wotquenne 50/1–6) and was followed up by two further groups of six which appeared in 1761 and 1763. These later sets are chronologically numbered 81–86 (Wotquenne 51/1–6) and 87–92 (Wotquenne 52/1–6). In addition to the German publications, John Walsh of Catherine Street in the Strand published the first and second sets but not the third.

The first group is now of especial interest because of an original edition which has entered the British Museum. This copy was evidently Bach's personal property, and presumably the one he used to play from. It contains a number of marginal alterations in the composer's own handwriting. A similar copy which has also passed through the composer's hands is lodged in the library of the Paris Conservatoire, and from a date on this copy (the last year of Bach's life) it seems that the precise time of the alterations can be ascertained.[4] There is yet another amended copy at Brussels. The sonatas with altered reprises have not been republished in modern times, although the fifth sonata, in its original version, is reprinted in an album of pieces published by Peters (Number 4188).

Sonatas contained in the collection of Sonatas, Free Fantasias and Rondos 'für Kenner und Liebhaber' ('Sonatas for Connoisseurs and Amateurs')

This collection consists of six volumes appearing respectively in 1779, 1780, 1781, 1783, 1785 and 1787. The first volume contains six sonatas (numbers 119–24 in list order and Wotquenne 55/1–6). So far as can be ascertained, these were composed in 1773, 1758, 1774, 1765, 1772 and 1765 respectively. Bach evidently grouped these works as a set for purposes of publication. He seems to have had a predilection for groups of six.

The second volume contains three sonatas, numbers 125–27 (Wotquenne 56/2, 56/4 and 56/6). These were probably composed in 1774, 1780 and 1780 respectively. Volume two appeared in 1780.

The third volume, published in 1781 has three more, numbers 128–30 (Wotquenne 57/2, 57/4 and 57/6). The dates of composition show how Bach's grouping of these works was somewhat arbitrary. They were written in 1774, 1766 and 1763 respectively.

The fourth volume (1783) contains only two sonatas, numbers 131 and 132 (Wotquenne 58/2 and 58/4), composed respectively in 1781 and 1765.

The fifth came out in 1785 and again has only two sonatas, numbers 136 and 135 (Wotquenne 59/1 and 59/3) which were composed in 1784.

The last volume appeared in 1787, the year before Emanuel Bach died, and has two sonatas, numbers 140 and 141 (Wotquenne 61/2 and 61/5) composed in 1785.

This completes the list of important sonata-collections. It will be readily appreciated that Bach's total output is really sandwiched between the 'Prussian' sonatas and the six sets for music-lovers and amateurs. The practice-pieces appended to the *Essay on Keyboard Performance* and the sets with altered reprises form a middle, and make it possible to estimate his contribution to sonata-composition and the nature of his artistic development and growth in this field.

Six Sonates pour le Clavecin, à l'usage des Dames ('Sonatas for Ladies')

These are compositions of great charm and delicacy and they have many points of interest. However, they can scarcely be considered of great importance in the history of the keyboard sonata, even though they are delightful as keyboard music. An appropriate place to discuss them will be the chapter dealing with Emanuel Bach's miscellaneous compositions. They are listed in Wotquenne's Catalogue as number 54 1/6, and are available in the edition *Mitteldeutscher Verlag*.

The Fantasias

As we shall see, the medium of the fantasia is a fundamental pillar of Bach's keyboard style. He discussed the subject of improvisation at length in the *Essay* and included a full-length example of a fantasia in the text. This is the Fantasia in D major written for the second part of the *Essay* published in 1762.

The most impressive fantasia composed by Bach for the clavichord was certainly the Fantasia in C minor which rounds off the *Probe-Stücke*. It affords us many important clues to the precise way in which Bach applied his own theories.

Possibly the most extended example of the free fantasia is the composition entitled *C. P. E. Bachs Empfindungen*. The original keyboard version was composed in 1787, and is thus an example of his maturest improvisatory style. There is a slightly later version for keyboard and violin which ends with a light allegro.

All the other fantasias with which we shall be concerned are contained in the six volumes of sonatas, rondos and fantasias for amateurs already listed. They are apportioned as follows:

Volume IV: Fantasia in E flat and Fantasia in A.

Volume V: Fantasia in F and Fantasia in C.

Volume VI: Fantasia in B flat and Fantasia in C – the last is a fantastic, kittenish piece of music which manages to be at once an astral parody of Domenico Scarlatti and an uncanny preview of first-period Beethoven.

Taken as a whole, these eight fantasias constitute a vitally important part of Emanuel Bach's output. It is my own opinion that his whole attitude to the art of improvisation, whether free or composed (as in a written fantasia) reveals as much about the man and his contribution to the history of music as the bulk of his sonata output. But of this more later.

The Rondos

The most famous is undoubtedly the *Abschied vom Silbermanschen Clavier* composed in August 1781.

Other extended pieces in this style are contained in the volumes for music-lovers and amateurs, apportioned as follows:

Volume II: Rondo in C, Rondo in D, Rondo in A minor.

Volume III: Rondo in E, Rondo in G, Rondo in F.

Volume IV: Rondo in A, Rondo in E, Rondo in B flat.

Volume V: Rondo in G, Rondo in C minor.

Volume VI: Rondo in E flat, Rondo in D minor.

Fugues

Bach's essays in a strictly contrapuntal idiom for solo keyboard (presumably organ, clavichord or harpsichord) consist of a duo in counterpoint at the octave, eleventh and twelfth, five fugues (D minor, F major, A major, G minor and E flat major), and a Fantasia and Fugue in C minor. These works were composed mainly for Marpurg's collections and one may be excused for feeling that they are conventional in style, and perhaps a little self-consciously academic. The feeling was already established that any claim to musicianship, whatever one's accomplishments in other genres, had to be substantiated by solid contrapuntal ability. The examination fugue is doubtless the *reductio* of this argument, which is sound enough in principle.

It does not seem enough to dismiss these compositions, as Geiringer does in his book *The Bach Family*, with a mere footnote indicating that they 'clearly display the composer's indifference towards the form of the instrumental fugue'. Accordingly I have selected three examples for consideration, and they will be found complete at the end of this book. If we are to consider Emanuel's solo keyboard music in the round, it seems reasonable to have a look at his fugues. Apart from that, they are not uninteresting works, and two of them at least (the fugues in A major and E flat) do not appear to have been reprinted since the eighteenth century. They are worth bringing to the notice of modern pianists and clavichordists.

The Fugue in D minor was included in Marpurg's *Fugen-Sammlung*, Volume I, published in Berlin in 1758. It was reprinted by Fétis (père) in the twelfth volume of his *Oeuvres Choisies* when he was director of the Conservatoire at Brussels.

The Fugue in A major appeared first in Marpurg's *Raccolta delle più nuove Composizioni di Cembalo di differenti Maestri ed Autori per l'anno 1757*, and subsequently in another collection of practice-pieces also edited by Marpurg; *Clavierstücke mit einem practischen Unterricht für Anfänger und Geübtere*, Berlin 1762. In this edition Marpurg added a running commentary to the musical text, explaining Bach's contrapuntal procedures.

The Fugue in E flat was included in the second volume of Marpurg's *Clavierstücke*, which also appeared in 1762.

Bach's five fugues, duo, and fantasia and fugue are grouped by Wotquenne as Opus 119, and the fugues in D minor, A major and E flat are respectively W. 119 numbers 2, 4 and 6.

Miscellaneous Pieces

C. P. E. Bach wrote many pieces for clavichord, harpsichord and early piano other than the fantasias, sonatas and rondos already noted. One of the most famous collections is entitled *Kurze und leichte Klavierstücke mit veränderten Reprisen* and was published in 1766 and 1768. Wotquenne listed the two parts of this collection 113 and 114. Otto Vrieslander subsequently reprinted it, and Heinrich Schenker exercised his analytical genius upon the first piece to reveal how the composer derived the entire composition from the most elementary motivic fragments. *Kurze und leichte Stücke* is now available in a modern edition (Wiener Urtext Ausgabe, Universal 13311) by Oswald Jonas. This is a scholarly and valuable production, and the editor's report, together with a table of ornaments, is separately available. The various albums and small collections which are available in other modern editions tend to draw upon the *Kurze und leichte Stücke*. This is especially true of the two volumes in the Chester Library, entitled *Eighteenth Century Music*, and containing music by W. F., J. C., and C. P. E. Bach. Other pieces to which reference will be made will be found in the following modern editions:

C. P. E. Bach. Clavierstücke, Universal Edition 11015.

Album of Pieces by C. P. E. Bach, Peters 4188.

Philip Emanuel Bach Klavierwerke, Critical Edition by H. Schenker. Un.548 a/b.

This consists exclusively of sonatas, odd movements and one rondo taken from the collection for music-lovers and amateurs. It is a useful guide for those who are baffled by Bach's elaborate ornamentation, and it includes most of the best sonata movements for the convenience of those who do not wish to purchase the six volumes described above.

This preliminary classification does not remotely claim to be exhaustive. It *is* claimed, however, that it represents the best approach to Emanuel Bach's keyboard music as a whole. All the best and most interesting music is represented herein. I am aiming at an assessment of Bach's achievement in the light of those works for which he is justly famed, and I believe that the highest levels of Bach's creative achievement, when considered in the light of his known aspirations and his expressed aesthetic theories, are a significant contribution to musical history and aesthetics, a contribution which, despite much critical and historical writing, has not yet been adequately or even correctly assessed.

A note on Instruments

This is perhaps the best place to add a word about the keyboard instruments most suitable for the works discussed in this book. Inevitably, most modern students of eighteenth century keyboard music will have to turn to the pianoforte when trying over musical examples. It should be pointed out that whereas some pieces by Emanuel Bach sound very well on the piano, many do not. An impression of thinness arising from slender textures, sparsely-harmonised recitative-like passages and arioso melody is heightened by the modern instrument but considerably diminished when such passages are played upon a clavichord. The fact is that C. P. E. Bach was devoted to the clavichord and it seems incontrovertible that he calculated his effects – especially his dynamics – with the clavichord primarily in mind.

Those unfamiliar with the German clavier tradition often naively suppose that all pre-pianoforte music was composed for the harpsichord. Laying aside such misapprehensions, we must nevertheless assume that a great deal of harpsichord music was probably played upon the clavichord, which was a much cheaper instrument and more widely relied upon in the home than its expensive cousin. The reverse was also the case, and it is certain that a harpsichordist would not scruple to avail himself of the repertoire available for the clavichord. This is equally true at the present time. Yet again, as the fortepiano became increasingly popular, there can be no doubt that the music originally composed for specific use on either harpsichord or clavichord would be freely played upon the new instrument. It is to Clementi, Hummel, J. L. Dusík and others that we owe a debt for providing a wealth of delightful music which exploits the distinctive characteristics of the early piano.

There are, of course, basic differences between harpsichord, clavichord and fortepiano which should never be ignored by modern performers concerned with recapturing the true spirit of Emanuel Bach's sonatas, rondos and fantasias. The harpsichord (as also the spinet and virginals) is a plucked string instrument. It is, in effect, a harp laid out flat, the strings being activated by a keyboard instead of directly by the fingers. It has, indeed, some affinity with the lute and guitar, and a skilled guitarist can imitate the sound of the harpsichord with striking results. The clavichord is constructed in quite a different way, the strings being sounded by a key which presses upon them directly. The initial sound is produced through the medium of a brass 'tangent' at the end of the key. A further important point underlines the relation of the clavichord to the mediaeval monochord. In the earlier clavichords, the point at which the tangent strikes the string also determines the mathematical length of vibrating string necessary to produce the required note. Later instruments exploit the increased resonance of a larger wooden case, and the greater tone derived from two or more strings to a note. The Silbermann instruments used by Emanuel Bach were of this type.

The fact that the tangent remains in contact with the string during the actual sounding of the note distinguishes it from all other keyboard instruments. In the pianoforte and harpsichord, the finger cannot influence the sounding tone in any way whatsoever once the key has been depressed. The pianoforte hammer falls back, leaving the string free to vibrate; the harpsichord quill is flicked to one side to produce the same result. In the clavichord, the finger can induce a vibrato effect by leaning or rocking on the key. This is the celebrated *Bebung* – imitated by Beethoven in the recitative section of the pianoforte sonata in A flat, opus 110. It is extremely difficult to achieve on a modern piano. *Bebung* must have played a vital part in the rendering of clavichord pieces in slow time, and in the performance of sustained notes generally. It is also very possible that this effect was as integral to the personal style of a clavichord player as the vibrato is to a modern violinist. Certainly the peculiar characteristics of the clavichord made it an apt solo medium for exploiting *Affektenlehre*, the doctrine of the affections.

The fortepiano gained in popularity during Emanuel Bach's life-time, and it is beyond doubt that the question as to whether a piece of keyboard music was to be played upon harpsichord, clavichord or forte-piano became a matter of personal preference as far as the average per-former was concerned. Perhaps the choice was also determined by fashion or social position, according to circumstance. Towards the end of the eighteenth century, a piece of solo keyboard music styled *für Clavier* was somewhat indifferently regarded as being suitable for any keyboard instrument in which the sound was produced by vibrating strings. Beethoven's early sonatas were evidently played on the harpsi-chord, and it is very likely that many of C. P. E. Bach's sonatas were also played on that instrument. However, to the discriminating modern ear, a harpsichord reading of Beethoven's first sonata would seem very in-congruous, and I cannot help feeling that by the same standards those very connoisseurs for whom Emanuel Bach composed his greatest col-lection of sonatas, rondos and fantasias would feel a harpsichord to be inappropriate.

It is significant that the 'Sonatas, Fantasias and Rondos for Con-noisseurs and Amateurs' are styled 'for fortepiano'. These works un-mistakably show the influence of the newer instrument, and it is interest-ing that some of the affecting passages in the sonatas of Muzio Clementi and J. L. Dusík for the piano show the impress of Emanuel Bach. In other words, there are some features of C. P. E. Bach's keyboard style which belong to the history of the piano as such, and which are accept-able even on a modern instrument.

At the same time, and this I feel to be profoundly important, it seems a mistake to take the designation 'for fortepiano' too seriously where the solo sonatas, fantasias and rondos are concerned. If a modern pianist-composer were to be confronted with a new type of keyboard instrument, working according to a new and unfamiliar principle, and producing a different quality of tone colour, he would, no doubt, eventually manage to compose music entirely appropriate to the new medium. But at first he would inevitably approach the new instrument with all the basic assumptions and presuppositions derived from his experience of tradi-tional instruments.

There are many works in the collections discussed in this book which bear out the same point. Played on a fortepiano they are reasonably acceptable. Played on a clavichord, with full use being made of the peculiarly introspective resources of that instrument, they reveal un-suspected beauties.

These remarks are not intended to amount to a dogmatic assertion that all Emanuel Bach's solo keyboard pieces should be played upon the clavichord. Far from it; but it is important that we should be aware of the deep relation which exists between Bach's theory of musical expression and the instrument he loved best of all. It is natural that a forward-looking and adventurous composer should wish to explore the possibilities of a new keyboard instrument. My point is that his best music for solo keyboard reveals the latent presuppositions of a clavichordist first and foremost. From time to time there are truly pianistic effects; but we seldom find the powerful octave doublings of a Hummel, the rippling and almost Chopinesque poetry of a Dusík, or the thundering *attacca* of a Clementi. Compared with these composers, C. P. E. Bach is a generation behind as far as pianoforte technique is concerned. At the same time, I do not wish to prejudice a fuller appraisal of the undoubtedly interesting writing for fortepiano found in his concertos for that instrument. My concern here is with the solo keyboard works.

In examining the legacy of C. P. E. Bach in the realm of solo keyboard music, I shall accept what I believe Emanuel's own presuppositions to have been; but when a work seems more suitable for performance upon an instrument other than the clavichord, I shall say so.

Chapter four

Improvisation and Fantasia

I N one vital sense, improvisation is the life-blood of music. Every interpretative act during performance, however carefully rehearsed, always
embodies an element of improvisation. The creative act is a present act,
and the lived moment of creative experience is always open to an in-
break, an uprush of uninhibited self-transcendence. One may have played
a piece hundreds of times in rehearsal. At the definitive moment of performance before an audience, some new vision, some new and powerful
inspiration can take over the hands, and the result is a more satisfying
experience of the music. Ideally, a performance is 'once-only'. Even the
performer who believes himself to be giving the identical interpretation
he always accords a certain work, deludes himself if he thinks that his
performances are not subject to variation according to fluctuations of
mood and feeling. Nature, in the structure of the human body and even
elevated to the dignity of human consciousness which cannot, after all,
be considered apart from nature, appears to abhor mere repetition as she
does vacuums. When the elements of difference are purely unconscious,
then the performer is limited by his inability to achieve absolute sameness – if a constant, unvarying interpretation of a given work is his
deliberate aim. But when he realizes that every performance really is a
unique creative act which can never be repeated in exactly the same
form, even though its impact can be remembered years afterwards, then
it is open to him to embrace the 'uncertainty principle' in performance,
and elevate it to the dignity of art, to transform it into a channel of
inspiration, to make it an open door through which an ever-fecundating
creative insight can flow.

The art of improvisation raises the 'uncertainty principle' to its
highest power. The born improviser is ever open to the inspiration of the
present moment; the 'now' is the immediate stimulus of what is to come.

This does not mean that every practical musician or composer is, or must be, skilled in the art; although his way through a musical career will be less difficult if he has the gift of improvisation, as Emanuel Bach points out in his *Versuch*. The point is rather that the very act of composition is at first an act of improvisation. The first sketches of a work, the first tentative drafts – these are a kind of improvisation in slow motion. Improvisation is essentially the first matter of musical thinking, the primary stuff which is later going to be shaped and informed by thought disciplined to a high degree of formal precision.

Perhaps we pay insufficient attention to the basic phenomenon of improvisation nowadays. Perhaps, in this age, we pay too much attention to analytical procedures instead of struggling to comprehend the compositional process and trying to stimulate its healthy growth. It is, after all, and especially to those who have no aptitude in this direction, a very remarkable thing to be able to pour out a stream of music spontaneously, with such a sense of immediacy that the hands do not so much follow the thought as live it from the very first moment of its generation. Improvisation is one of the real mysteries of artistic creation. It is recorded that many Buddhist and Taoist painters worked with lightning speed and precision, to produce pictures of an unparalleled mystical intensity. When we remember that painting was regarded as a branch of calligraphy by these geniuses of the Tang and Sung dynasties, we can more readily see how subjective image and hand worked together in a spontaneous harmony.

A deeper and more relevant point is that their pictures expressed at once an objective scene and a state of subjective being, and that in contemplating them the mind is in effect being absorbed by the objective pattern and the subjective state which conceived it. This condition of subjective being was the positive or inward end of a psycho-physical complex. Oriental pictures are frequently 'pictures of consciousness'.

Dr Burney,[1] in a famous passage which has been frequently quoted, describes how Emanuel Bach entertained him until far into the night at his clavichord. We learn how the composer made his instrument sing, how he vividly lived the emotions he was transmuting into tone, how indeed, he perspired with the intensity of his concentration.

Burney's description suggests one thing quite clearly. A certain amount of mental effort went into Bach's performance. Because of this we should beware of likening Bach's improvisatory skill to the oriental type referred to above. The Tang painters, not unlike the action painters of our own day, seemed to work in the twinkling of an eye, without much conscious effort. Professor Suzuki has offered an explanation of this[2] – namely, that whereas the Western mind is rooted in the principle of consciousness, the Oriental is in a much more spontaneous *rapport* with the unconscious.

In the West, artistic creation often seems to be a wresting of form from mass rather than a spontaneous blossoming. Nevertheless, the underlying principle of spontaneity can be observed in Western, as in Oriental art.

The measure of spontaneity in Bach's own improvisations can perhaps partly be judged by the simple test of trying to do likewise ourselves. How confidently can we rely upon our musical inwardness to flow outwards through our hands? How certain can we be of the musical value of the results? And if it were true that Bach simply thought more quickly, and gained the power to order his effects consciously, then how quickly can we think, and how much power have we gained to order our effects in accordance with some readily appreciated aesthetic design? The mind which has real skill in improvisation has perhaps much in common with the mind which can add up a fantastic column of figures in a second or two, or the mind which always sees the winning pattern at chess. Indeed, it seems permissible to arrange arithmetic, chess and musical improvisation in a crescendo of significance. Addition of a long series of complex numbers is fundamentally mechanical. Chess is mechanics raised to a higher power by thought and a certain sense of aesthetic fitness,[3] whereas improvisation demands spontaneous mechanism, thought and imagination. The ultimate act of improvisation, which produces results of real aesthetic value, is a kind of musical intuition in which kinesis, thought, imagination and will coalesce into a unity. Ability in improvisation presupposes a high degree of musical integration. If we have not this ability, we should not shrink from the truth that we are the poorer as musicians.

Fortunately, Emanuel Bach has left us clear evidence about his own methods. To many contemporary listeners, no doubt, Bach was a composer and skilled clavichordist who could sit down at his instrument and pour out a stream of attractive figuration, dramatic harmony and soul-stirring melody. We can be sure that he already had a stock of musical devices, and that he worked according to a plan – one already built into his musical consciousness, or one quickly formulated for the occasion. In the *Versuch*, there is a revealing chapter on improvisation which is still of great value in helping the student to develop skill in the art, and which underlines its essential principles with scientific precision. It is in this chapter that we discern the cool intellect behind the philosophy of the affections.

Bach is explicitly concerned with the Free Fantasia, and by this he does not mean the merely extempore flourish with which a performer impressed his audience before settling down to play a composed work:

'There are occasions when an accompanist must extemporise before the beginning of a piece. Because such an improvisation is to be

regarded as a prelude which prepares the listener for the content of
the piece that follows, it is more restricted than the fantasia, from
which nothing more is required than a display of the keyboardist's
skill. The construction of the former is determined by the nature of
the piece which it prefaces; and the content or affect of this piece
becomes the material out of which the prelude is fashioned. But in a
fantasia the performer is completely free, there being no attendant
restrictions.'[4]

Obviously, the free fantasia requires a considerable knowledge of
composition. Bach predicted a good future in composition for anyone who
could improvise and who wrote profusely – without, he added, starting
too late. One wonders, in parenthesis, whether the wisdom of Bach in this
fundamental matter has not been completely overridden by the system of
musical education characteristic of our own country at the present time.

In accordance with accepted practice, Bach recommends the keyboardist to begin his study with simple harmonies added to ascending and
descending forms of the major and minor scales. These can be arpeggiated, played with alternate dramatic effects of forte and piano, inter-
spersed with passage-work, extended with figuration orientated around a
particular chord or progression and generally spread in musical time-
space[5] in as varied and interesting a manner as possible. Here are some of
Bach's simplest examples:

EX. I

An obvious caution is that the tonic key must be firmly established at
the beginning and end, and that modulation must be adjusted to the
time-scale, remote modulation being acceptable only in a long fantasia.
At the end of the scalic progression, return to the dominant for an extended cadence is a formal requisite which can sometimes be dispensed with.
The penultimate chord can be a seventh, sixth or six-five taken above the
leading-note.

As greater proficiency is gained, the performer can indulge in 'feigned
modulation' and 'rational deceptions'; but these must not be excessively
used or natural relationships will become hopelessly buried beneath them.
Again, chromaticism is a useful aid to variety but must be played with
artistry, and broadly.

Eventually, by interpolating chromatic notes into the diatonic scale series, and by displacing or repeating certain notes, a true compositional matrix may be arrived at. An example of such a matrix, taken from the examples given by Bach in the *Versuch*, is given below:

EX. 2

The matrix is the first degree of the form of a free fantasia. It can be preconceived, and carried in a mental pigeon-hole ready for instant use at a concert, or it may be quickly thought up as the performer walks to his seat at the instrument upon which he is going to improvise. Or, alternatively, it can be consciously evolved in the very act of performance. Psychologically speaking, there appears to be a difference between sitting down to improvise upon a bass previously conceived and thinking one up as one goes along. The latter procedure is more spontaneous, more obviously improvisatory. But there is plenty of opportunity, even in the former case, for the free and spontaneous emergence of inspired musical thought. Indeed, one may be sure that in Bach's own case, the dispassionately-conceived matrix was frequently dissolved in a rhapsodic flow which took quite a different course from that perhaps originally intended. Again, one feels that if this ever happens in any act of improvisation, then it is all to the good. It seems permissible to interpret Bach's injunctions with a certain freedom, to accept all his teachings as good, but more as intellectual preliminaries to truly spontaneous musical thought. And one feels that Bach would find nothing to cavil at in this.

If the musical mind were little more than a dispassionate intellect thinking coldly with sounds instead of linguistic relations then, indeed, his remarks on improvisation, bearing in mind the restricted harmonic idiom of his day, would be the last word on the art. But they are not the last word, as Bach insisted. Indeed, he strenuously supported a musical aesthetic which stressed that far from being the cold conception of musical form, the whole procedure of composition served the ends of subjective expression. A few quotations from the *Versuch* will bear this out:

'The beauty of variety is made evident in the fantasia. A diversified figuration and all attributes of good performance must be employed. The ear tires of unrelieved passage-work, sustained chords, or broken chords. By themselves they neither stir nor still the passions; and it is for these purposes that the fantasia is exceptionally well suited.' (Mitchell's translation, p. 438–9.)

'A musician cannot move others unless he too is moved. He must of necessity feel all of the effects that he hopes to arouse in his audience, for the revealing of his own humour will stimulate a like humour in the listener. In languishing, sad passages, the performer must languish and grow sad. . . . Similarly, in lively, joyous passages the executant must again put himself into the appropriate mood. And so, constantly varying the passions he will barely quiet one before he rouses another.' (Op. cit., p. 152.)

This passage is of course liable to misinterpretation, and it opens the door to charlatanism. It is unfortunately all too possible to impress an audience with one's mannerisms and expression rather than with one's musicianship. Emanuel Bach cannot be entirely exonerated from blame. He is, in a certain sense, the father of the 'agonized expression' school. However, there can be no doubt that his aesthetic aims were genuine. He would certainly have been the last to tolerate inadequate musicianship however sincerely a musician experienced the emotions he was trying to communicate to his audience.

'. . . it is especially in fantasias, those expressions not of memorized or plagiarized passages, but rather of true musical creativeness, that the keyboardist more than any other executant can practice the declamatory style, and move audaciously from one affect to the other.'

In pursuit of the idea of unfettered keyboard declamation, recitative in which the positive, subjective urge is pushed to the utmost, Bach himself played 'without bar-lines' and passages in his written-out fantasias frequently have no formal metrical arrangement.

Here is a powerful example from the 'Hamlet' Fantasia, the last of the *Probe-Stücke*:

EX. 3

In order to understand how such passages came to be written for the keyboard, we have to take account of a number of influential factors. The most important is the dramatic tradition associated with the development of recitative in opera, and subsequently in oratorios and cantatas; almost equally important is the aesthetic of *Empfindsamkeit*. Obviously there is a powerful ingredient which the earlier dramatic theory has in common with the more supple and refined attitude towards 'the passions' characteristic of the middle eighteenth century. *Empfindsamkeit* denotes the appreciation of a larger psychological truth, namely that the soul not only has 'passions', but that there is a sense in which these passions have rhythm and connectedness, a kind of unconscious logic.

The unconscious has been defined as 'consciousness without the ego'. This is illuminating in relation to the psychological basis of *Empfind-samkeit* as it was understood by Bach. Furthermore, it needs to be considered in relation to the root meaning of the word passion. Passion is suffering, the experience of forces either imposed from without or arising spontaneously within the soul. The unconscious is then the arena of passion, the realm where forces either register their impact or even have their origin. The idea of passions welling up from the unconscious into the sphere of consciousness is a real one. *Empfindsamkeit* recognizes the fact that passion is a basic substratum of human experience, and that this substratum is not by any means a *tabula rasa* but a heaving sea of restless affection and disaffection. The addition of the ego-principle to this heaving sea is virtually the addition of the contemplative intellect, which can now register, identify and name the contending forces upon which it strives to impose some sort of order and discipline.

We arrive at the idea that unconsciousness (awareness without ego) is the basis of what consciousness can mould into a definite order. *Empfind-samkeit* really asserts consciousness over against unconsciousness in so far as it is nothing less than a theory consciously formulated and critically discussed. It was a prime talking-point amongst Emanuel Bach and his Berlin associates, Marpurg, Kirnberger, Quantz and the others.

The deliberate and direct simulation of the passions in a free fantasia, by the calculated progression of chords, arpeggios, runs, modulations, accented passing-notes and so on is the objective polarity of a psycho-physical complex characterized by a subjective undulation of feeling. This subjective undulation, this flow of *Affekte*, was rationally objectified, theorized about and elevated to the status of musical art. It was eventually taken completely for granted. Indeed, those who instinctively say 'Music is expression' when asked to define the art, are true descendants of this aesthetic school.

Important points must be made here in order to place Bach in his proper perspective not only in the history of music, but also in the wider context of the history of Aesthetic.

Firstly, Emanuel's keyboard recitative had had its forerunners, although these seldom rose to the uninhibited expressiveness of Bach's work. J. S. Bach's Chromatic Fantasia contains fine examples, and Kuhnau had also written in a recitative style:

EX. 4

Secondly, the theory of the affections, generally considered, is somewhat philosophically crude, and not much more than an offshoot of naturalism, the view that art is the imitation of nature, nature, in this case, being the raw stuff of human experience. This was the doctrine stated by Scheibe in *Der critische Musicus* in 1745. Indeed, the philosopher Winckelmann (1717–68), who maintained a point of view very close to that outlined in chapter two, that the study of workmanship brings us into direct contact with the human mind, and through this into the wider horizons of human consciousness, held that Beauty and Expression were actually opposed. In actual fact, and as Bosanquet pointed out, Winckelmann was 'too honest and accurate an observer of Greek sculpture' to maintain this bare opposition in the face of what his own sensibility proclaimed; but by elevating the opposition to the level of paradox he underlined a point profoundly relevant to our study. It is a fact that the word 'Beauty' is not mentioned frequently by Emanuel Bach in the *Versuch*, and that the underlying notion of Expression is paramount. Expression deals with the concrete stuff of experience. Beauty, on the other hand, can be pushed to the limits of the transcendental, so that it becomes little more than an ethereal idea, a geometrical essence of motionless purity which must necessarily seem unreal or even antagonistic to a composer struggling to make his soul tonally articulate. But we owe to Winckelmann the further development of his own paradox, namely that Expression, which in principle is opposed to Beauty, yet 'reaches its maximum in the style of which Beauty is the distinctive attribute'.[6] This hints at a synthesis in which an objective and transcendent ideal of Beauty and an immanent, subjective emotional force not only coexist but interpenetrate – the result being a beautiful form which is emotionally articulate and which yet reduces us to a contemplative wonderment. Is not such a synthesis achieved in the music of Mozart, and is it going too far to see, in his work, the whole dynamic of *Empfindsamkeit* reduced to its proper proportions in a containing perfection of tonal order? This, perhaps, is to anticipate a little; but I believe there is a sense in which Emanuel Bach grasped the vital necessity of a principle of order which at once vindicated and disciplined the psychological basis of his work. In so far as he built a bridge between subjective and objective, inner and outer, Expression and Beauty, he is a powerful force in the development of what later came to be called 'the classical style'.

However, in the fantasias, we are bound to feel that Bach is far more concerned with a naturalism of the emotions, and this concern brings him more into line with the romantic principle, as it is popularly understood, than with the classical theorizing more characteristic of his contemporary aestheticians.

We should remember that Plato and Aristotle knew something about the expressive power of music, and were even dubious about it on that account. Aristotle, in particular, believed music to embody the very essence of emotion precisely because it had the power to arouse it. Particular tunes stimulate particular forms of excitement.[7] Bernard Bosanquet[8] considered Aristotle to be saying, in effect, that the movement of music, the actual flow of tones, is the very movement of the mind and heart in the person listening. Sometimes, in reading classical sources, one is made to feel that there is nothing new under the sun where aesthetic theory is concerned. Could there be a neater *résumé* of Bach's own view?

The dramatic potentialities of the passions, when expressed by the human voice, were first consciously emphasized by the Italians. The instrumental *rationale* of subjective declamation seems to have been achieved pre-eminently by the German clavier-composers. And this is the place to state that if the philosophical theory of the naturalistic expression of emotion seems crude compared with the more idealistic reflections of Baumgarten, Winckelmann and others, it seems to vindicate itself when passed through the refining fires of the musical imagination. As the theory of the passions moved farther north, it lost something of its vocal dynamic, and became universalized through the abstract medium of instrumental tone. What was individual and particular and extrovert in the Italian temperament became universal and ideal in the German, and not a little introspective as well. From the shrill and colourful exhibitionism of the Italian stage, wherein the individual achieved a kind of personalistic enlargement through song, the sphere of the passions achieved idealization in the muted tones of the clavichord. All the magic of subjective evocation was rediscovered when it was realized that the hands could sing as well as the voice, and that the clavichord especially, with its sobbing effects and vibrating *Bebung* could be a fitting medium for the *Affekte*. It is salutary to remember that the familiar notion of dramatic, expressive performance, which is now so much taken for granted, had once to emerge, to be discovered, to evolve, and that there was once a time when keyboard *Empfindsamkeit* was unknown. That it was once unknown to the keyboard-player we can deduce from the nature of early keyboard music which seems, in the main, to be primarily patternistic. But now let us see how *Empfindsamkeit* is applied in practice by a study of the 'Hamlet' Fantasia.

This remarkable composition falls into three sections. The first and last are freely rhapsodic, and are written out without bar-lines; the middle portion, built up around the key of E flat, the relative major, is barred yet very free in style – its main melodic thread:

EX. 5

being no more than a generating statement for a series of dramatic modulations:

EX. 6

The phrase 'generating statement' introduces a concept which is useful for a full appreciation of Bach's keyboard style. It denotes an extended thematic/harmonic figuration carrying a powerful emotional impetus, and it is, in effect, the central psycho-tonal nucleus of an *Affekt*. In analysing a generating statement we arrive at smaller units — 'moments' or 'quanta' comprehended by the *Affekt*, which are expressed in dramatic twists of figuration, individual fragments of harmony, or even moments of silence pregnant with expressive intention. The generating power of a group of such moments usually seems to spend itself in a flow of ideas which are rather like branches stemming from a main trunk. They may even repeat important thematic configurations which appeared in the main generating statement. It is acknowledged that this terminology has a somewhat arbitrary flavour; but it will serve to impose some kind of analytical order upon music which is not fundamentally patternistic and which has a profoundly inward reference. The first section of the C minor fantasia could then be regarded in this way:

Fantasia

The opening flourish is no more than an arpeggio in C minor; but an arpeggio thus sounded always makes a strong and challenging beginning if played with conviction, or a ruminative and pregnant introduction if played softly. Consider, for example, the opening of Beethoven's Sonata in D minor, opus 31, no. 2. Such beginnings have their ancestry in the keyboard fantasias of Froberger. The first generating statement, A–B is of course the generation of the whole piece, and so has an unique formal position. Subsidiary moments of this nucleus depend for their force upon the imagination of the player; but it is quite obvious that the long semi-quaver phrase must be played in such a way as to heighten its implied phraseology, and not rattled through with a flat equality of note-values. B–C is an extension period repeating the important descending seventh A flat – B natural, and it is basically contained within the chord of the diminished seventh. C–D is the next generating statement. It opens with a run in demi-semiquavers, and touches off a passage in slower notes which has many expressive turns of phrase. From here until the end of the piece, we find that a fast run is invariably followed by a slower and more ruminating flow. D–E is a longer period of extension which unfolds with a sense of climax. Bach then takes up a completely new idea, repeated on a basis of sevenths, dominant and diminished. The generating statement is obviously E-F, F-G being a modulatory extension, and ending with the cadence in G minor. The generally inconclusive sound of this cadence, however, prepares one for the next generating statement G-H, which touches off an ornamented extension H-I, repeating the cadence-figure, but this time without harmonic thickening.

In this last phrase, Bach seems to be deliberately exploiting a keyboard effect which fascinated Beethoven also in his last period. This is the separation of treble and bass by a considerable amount of keyboard space, and the meditative contemplation of the thin and tenuous sounds which result therefrom. The most famous example in Beethoven's music is the passage immediately following the trill in the middle of the last movement of opus 111.

The largo which follows, part of which has already been quoted, brings an altogether richer harmonic texture, and thus makes a necessary contrast with the whole of the preceding section. Bach takes the dominant note, B flat, vibrates an expressive *Bebung* upon it, sounds a clanging chord C-G-C in the bass, and then demonstrates the power of enharmonic modulation by proceeding to treat B flat as A sharp. The resulting flow of modulations leads to a final cadenza and a powerful, thickly-harmonized conclusion.

The fantasia is throughout a compelling and thought-provoking composition, amply worth the serious study of modern clavichordists, and perfectly convincing on a modern pianoforte. As it is a demonstration-piece intended to stimulate original improvisation in the style, there seems to be no point in refusing to avail oneself of the powerful dynamic range of the pianoforte. The fantasia can be built up into a dramatic *tour de force*. One wonders if Busoni knew the work. There can be no room for speculation about the way he would have treated it![9]

The overall structure is ternary. Schenker would view this as a prolongation of the progression I-III-I in C minor. He analyses the D major Fantasia included in the *Versuch*, but is more concerned to show how the modulations are enhanced presentations of this or that chord than true changes of centre.[10]

Bach is insistent that a fantasia is, *par excellence*, an opportunity for diversity of modulation. This might be the best place to deal briefly with Schenker's position since it bears upon important points which must appear throughout this book.

Schenker, and Adele Katz after him,[11] maintain that what conventional musical analysis considers fundamental modulations are really prolongations of basic harmonic relationships within the key. Thus a piece in C major, which modulates to the dominant and then back again to C major, is really a prolongation of a basic cadence I-V-I within C major. Ideally, no fundamental modulation is really involved and the piece never departs from the centrality of C major. Any other incidental modulations would not be changes of key either. They would be explained as enhancements of chords. His view is well known and it is unnecessary to restate it in detail here.

But a fundamental point must be made at once. The basic facts of musical experience are not altered by the language we use to describe them. Modulation is a phenomenon wherein nothing is added to the tonal essence by a technical vocabulary. The tonal essence is a series of subjectively experienced sounds unaffected by harmonic explanations—as, indeed, the opening of *Tristan* is neither more nor less affecting in view of all the different harmonic explanations which have been forwarded by theorists.

There is an elusive relativity about different schemes of harmonic analysis. They are frames imposed upon experience which help us to think intelligently about that experience. And that seems to be the end of the matter – until we turn to consider music as a psycho-physical reality. It is then that we come within range of significant explanation and description. Those who do not understand music as psycho-physical reality condemn themselves to the sphere of linguistic relativity – like those critics who appear to be obsessed with the visual appearance of musical scores and minor problems of intonation and interpretation.

To make this point a little clearer, let us consider the following example: a radio station may be perfectly or imperfectly tuned-in depending upon relative positions of a variable condenser. Thus, there are different aural experiences in this case symbolically indicated by relative positions of a needle on a numbered dial. The station is either tuned or mistuned, and positively known to be such in our experience. The dial positions are symbolic explanations of the various tuning positions. There is one point which is right, in relation to which all other points shade off into varying degrees of wrongness.

Now in the case of a given harmonic progression, assuming the instrument on which it is played to be properly constructed and tuned, only one tonal phenomenon is involved. There are no relative degrees of this phenomenon which invite different explanations. If different explanations are offered, they can never refer to anything else but this single phenomenon. Moreover, the criterion by which these different explanations are judged cannot be the simple one of truth or falsity. We must substitute the less precise one of general adequacy with regard to the experienced sounds. The reference must always be to experience. This is the scientific attitude, apart from everything else. Considerations advanced on a purely ideal basis may compel our interest and respect; but we must be most hospitable to those which do the most honour to our musical sensations.

Musical notation is the only adequate symbolic means of indicating the nature of a tonal event with anything like precision; but it can be ambiguous. This means that all verbal explanations based on musical notation tend to be less explanations of heard sounds than merely verbal structures woven around patterns of visual symbols. This relativity of the language of harmonic analysis does not seem to me to be sufficiently appreciated by Schenker and Katz, both of whom attempted to dogmatize about musical procedures. In actual fact, this is just one specialized application of a point of view which applies to linguistic explanation in general, and musicology must take note of it. There is a tendency for musicologists to write about music with a high disregard for the results of philosophical and linguistic analysis which have been arrived at in this present century. Musicologists and music critics, more than most perhaps, need to be aware of this, because anyone who has to write about music is all the time grappling with intangible and seemingly ideal elements. The unwary critic is all too prone to fall into the trap of writing about symbolic notation and not about music.

When we say, then, of a single progression: 'This is a modulation from tonic to dominant and back', or, 'This is a prolongation of the cadence I-V-I', in what sense is either statement true or false? This is a problem we must form a clear idea about, because the concept of modulation is really fundamental to the musical procedures and aesthetic theory of C. P. E. Bach. Upon it, his most significant musical thinking depends. His psychological aesthetic is based upon the notion of a real shift of tonal centre, and the contrast and opposition of keys.

Bearing in mind the relativity of verbal descriptions of objective phenomena, we must nevertheless recognize that there is a difference between (a) the various explanations which are respectively correlative with different phenomena (or different degrees of a single phenomenon), and (b) the different explanations which are offered of a single unvarying phenomenon like a fundamental harmonic progression. The word 'modulation' is vitiated, reduced to a lower level of significance, by the kind of harmonic analysis advocated by Schenker, plausible as Schenker's system seems to be. In music there is a basic experience which demands its own word. This experience is the disturbing apprehension of psycho-tonal polarity, a sense of subjective upheaval and dislocation of centre which is correlative with, and which seems to adjust itself spontaneously to fundamental deviations in the direction of the tonal flow. This can perhaps be illustrated with a telling example from Beethoven's Ninth Symphony:

EX. 8

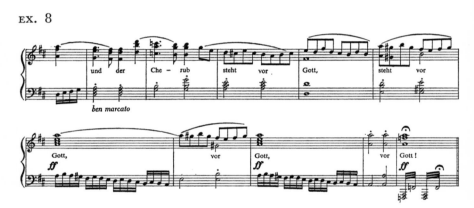

It would seem perverse to adopt a verbal explanation which, in the interests of a specious conception of harmonic unity, seeks to explain the F major chord as a fundamental ingredient of D major. The whole point of the passage is manifestly to dislocate the sense of D major, to break through into a new level of tonal apprehension; in other words – to create a sense of psycho-tonal polarity, in which the emphasis is not upon harmonic unity but vital differences in the scheme of things. Human feelings are as much a part of the scheme of things as sticks and stones and other 'objective realities'. Music, in fact, is their objectification; and modulation is a necessary means. It is precisely this kind of break-through which is consciously sought after by C. P. E. Bach in his fantasias. The very sound of the following passages is far more revealing than any verbal description. But if we seek verbal description, then the attitude of mind indicated by these examples surely inclines us to the traditional system of analysis which sees these surprising progressions as true modulations, changes of key, alterations of mode?

EXX. 9, 10, 11, 12, 13, 14

These examples are, incidentally, excellent pointers to Bach's keyboard mannerisms. It is not difficult to imagine how he would *look* in the act of performing such passages.

It is suggested, then, that the word *modulation*, as it is conventionally used, denotes a true assertion of psycho-tonal polarity, the establishment of conflicting tonal centres which are the outward, tonal signs of an inward awareness of conflicting emotions in the subjective consciousness.

Let us look a little farther into the matter. There we shall find some support for the traditional concept of modulation. If we suppose that modulation originally meant *change of mode*, or more generally, a simple rise and fall in tonal orientation, then we must determine what we mean by the word *mode*. It could be that some original content affords a useful clue to later usage. Indeed, words often seem to build up an 'unconscious' force of meaning, even as their official meaning deteriorates and thins out.

It seems reasonably established[12] that certain groupings of sounds had, in the prehistory of music, magical effects. This is to say that certain tonal orders could be systematically used to produce specific psychical changes. There is a close link between primitive incantations undertaken for magical purposes, and liturgical singing undertaken for spiritual ones. A man could be 'enchanted' by the repetition of certain intervals at a certain pitch. Changes of interval-relationship and pitch produced appropriate subjective modifications. (What is now called musical therapy is doubtless little more than a respectable rediscovery of the vital relationship between sound and the psyche.) In the formative days of plain-chant, different modes were felt to be appropriate to different liturgical functions.[13] With growing intellectual refinements, and the consequent enhancement of musical consciousness, as distinct from the musical unconscious which is frequently the gateway to less-desirable influences and activities, the more obvious psychical impacts were lost. This loss of the psychic values, which was, from the standpoint of musical art, a purging-away of non-musical associations, is reflected in a theoretical preoccupation with modal considerations from the tenth to the fifteenth centuries. Eventually, modal theory became a matter of *purely tonal relationships*. With equal temperament and the final codification of the major-minor scale system, the conscious objectification and emancipation of harmonic relationships becomes complete.

It is therefore all the more interesting to observe Emanuel Bach, in the eighteenth century, moving over to the subjective antithesis, upholding the emotional force of harmony, and stressing the expressive variety to be gained from change of key. But now we see a kind of complete inversion. The old magicians and priest-musicians manipulated sound to gain psychical control over the minds of their victims or worshippers. Bach, fully realizing that to move others one must oneself be moved, and that one must first learn the technical craft of musical expression, condenses the idea of the subjective impulse into a philosophical concept. This further objectification of the subjective sphere of musical experience is of vital significance in musical history. It represents a real advance of the musical consciousness in general, and underlines the real basis of the classical impulse in the great period of Austro-German music. Classicism is not the negation of emotional expression, but its objectification. This objectification finds its manifestation in a modulating framework which, at a later stage, is objectively disciplined by that dialectical manner of tonal thinking comprehended by the phrase 'sonata-principle'.

It will be worth considering, at this point, the specific usage of the word 'objectification' in the above paragraph, with reference to the Hegelian concept of *negation*. In the philosophy of Hegel, the term *negation* denotes, in a special sense, the objectification or cancelling-out of a subjective content so that it can be 'formed' or 'projected'. What is purely subjective is nascent; what is objective is a condition of subjectivity turned into a shape or presentation to consciousness. Bach, in the *Versuch*, is obviously advocating something like this. One must *feel*; one must 'emote'; one must express on one's features the agony of one's soul. At the same time, one must be a true musician, a master of the craft of notes, able to achieve a technical *rationale* in the outwardness of tone of all that takes place within. As an artist, Bach is in the end more concerned with the outwardness, the finished, objective product, the shape of the thing. But we must always bear in mind the conscious twofold antithesis, the process of transmutation from feeling to form, the emergence or self-stimulating creation of an inwardness, a positive psychological urge and its negation in the outward. The result is a true synthesis, a psycho-tonal wholeness in which form and matter are indissolubly fused. And this psycho-tonal wholeness, as far as the fantasias are concerned, is a fluid structure freely evolving around conflicting key-centres. This fluid structure is nothing less than the logically prior 'stuff' which, at another level of musical development, is transformed by the sonata-principle.

We are now in a position to summarize Emanuel Bach's aesthetic in relation to the fantasia: it is in a fantasia that the performer gives expression to the *Affekte*. In such expression, passages which are sharply contrasted in terms of melodic structure and tonal centre are fundamental. His general procedure is to make a number of generating statements which respectively embody dynamic *Affekte*. These spend themselves branchwise in a freely rhapsodic flow and may involve a number of modulations. Generating statements are the tonal form of subjective impulsions, whether heartfelt throbs of the psyche or whimsical moments of more superficial feeling, and they tend to establish themselves as individual and personal. They polarize themselves. The wayward flow of consciousness, the backcloth of awareness, is heightened and intensified during the creative process. The subjective stream breaks up into a number of polarized centres, particles of positive consciousness, so to speak, which then seek their appropriate outward form in rhythms, melody and harmony. The rest, too, is an especially significant element of tonal thought from the standpoint of *Empfindsamkeit*, since it underlines the intrinsic, individual and polarized quality of moments of musically charged feeling by separating them. It also established itself as such a moment. In the Bach fantasia, these separate elements, these bundles of polarized centres are the ultimate determinants of a modulation-scheme. Even if a modulation-scheme is worked out beforehand, from a preconceived bass-line, its musical justification will depend upon its interior drive, its psychological integrity.

To provide further illustration of the points made in this chapter, the next will be devoted to a discussion of the Fantasia in E flat (SKL IV). A detailed analysis of the Fantasia 'C. P. E. Bachs Empfindungen' has already appeared in print.[14]

Chapter five

The Fantasia in E flat major (SKL IV)

THIS work is well worth a serious performance by modern pianists or neo-clavichordists. It is an astonishing compendium of keyboard devices – some of them traditional, some in line with the (then) contemporary fashion, and some definitely futuristic. Looked at historically, the imaginative 'spread' of the music seems quite fantastic at times, even grotesque; and the bulk of Mozart's music for keyboard, which of course reveals a much higher degree of tonal organization, is generally less remarkable than this. The work gives force to the idea, already discussed,[1] that Emanuel Bach represents a new kind of consciousness in music. His music is a theatre in which an almost grotesque and heterogeneous association of elements is manifesting itself in a state of turbulence. It demands a new order of organization, a new principle, a new kind of *rapprochement* between the inner consciousness and the outer form. In this fantasia, seventeenth-, eighteenth- and even nineteenth-century elements jostle together – not in order that one may gain supremacy, but collectively with an invitation to their interior psychological and exterior formal integration.

This is immediately apparent from EX. 15a, with which the fantasia begins:

EX. 15a

The arpeggiation of the first line is more characteristic of the early nineteenth century than it is of Bach's time. A very similar pattern may be seen in Weber's Sonata in A flat:

EX. 15b

The Bach passage quoted is the first generating statement of the fantasia. It is immediately extended by further figuration on the chord of A flat, a diminished seventh, and a final dominant-tonic arpeggiation. All this amounts to no more than an ebullient presentation of the key of E flat (as in the opening of Beethoven's Fifth Pianoforte Concerto); but after a short rest a violent semiquaver passage hurls the music into B flat minor. This modulating link has a remarkably Beethoven-like character, and seems to demand not only a powerful attacca but considerably more tone than the clavichord can make available. In this case a fortepiano or even a modern pianoforte would be the better instrument.

EX. 16

The passage which follows has already been quoted (EX. 10). It has a recitative-flavour, and is built up mainly on chords of the sixth in ascending order. This ascending movement brings a scalic outline into prominence in both treble and bass:

EXX . 17a, b

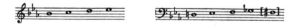

and subsequently

EX. 17c

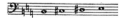

which forms the bass to a wandering passage in triplets. This tails off almost haphazardly into more arpeggios which are to be played *ad lib* over a figured bass. Bach gives only the bass – his custom in such passages – but the chordal progression implied is forceful and dramatic:

EX. 18

This leads back to the opening pattern of figuration, somewhat modified, and reaches a cadence in A minor. Analysis of the fantasia thus far suggests that it is constructed upon the following bass-line:

EX. 19

The formal effect is clear A-B-A, the A part being the first generating arpeggio statement, the B being EX. 10, and the two being linked by the short modulating passage EX. 16. The scalic passage referred to above is really contained in the ground-plan.

The long 'poco adagio' which now follows is based upon a syncopated theme:

EX. 20

which, in its subsequent extensions is accompanied by descending scalewise figures which are possibly unconscious versions of EX. 17. It would be going too far to suggest that these are deliberate manipulations of anything akin to a serial form; but they are quite likely to be reflections of an underlying tendency:

EX. 21

and

In some places, the bass-line becomes 'atmospheric' rather than formal:

EX. 22

and this suggests that the notion of a ground-plan has been abandoned in favour of an unfettered, ruminating and mysterious soliloquy owing little or nothing to conscious constructivism. The whole of this adagio throbs and pulsates in a most disturbing fashion; it is difficult to believe that it belongs to the same work as EX. 15a. It finally dissolves into more allegro arpeggiation which is closely related to the opening of the fantasia:

EX. 23

When this finally reaches a half-close in E flat, EX. 10 is restated in full, and then followed by a developed and extended version of EX. 16 which originally preceded it. The opening statement, exactly as originally written, follows without a break and brings the fantasia to a conclusion.

The overall form of the fantasia is thus cyclical. It could be regarded as a very loose rondo, or alternatively as an exposition and recapitulation with an interpolated adagio in a remote key instead of a 'development':

Allegro	A section	E flat
	B section	B flat minor over EX. 19
	A repeated	G major to A minor
Adagio	C section	A minor, with frequent modulation
Allegro	A modified, leading to	
	B	E flat minor
	A	A flat major, and literal restatement of opening.

The purpose of this analysis is not to create the impression that the fantasia is an essay in a free kind of sonata-form, or is revelatory of the rise of sonata-form. After all, C. P. E. Bach had by this time composed the bulk of his sonata output, on which the traditional claim that he was the true 'father of sonata-form' rests. The point is somewhat more subtle than this. What is really important is the cyclical arrangement which emerges on the basis of such disparate and contrasting tonal elements. The question we should ask is this: Was the cyclical order imposed from without, intellectually or arbitrarily, or was it an unconscious response of Bach's creative mind to the impact of a dramatic heterogeneity? In other words, where the creative consciousness confronts itself, or is confronted with a mass of disparate material, does it instinctively tend to order this on a basis of statement, extension and restatement with respect to key-relationships or thematic structure? I think it is more important to ask this question than to attempt a definitive answer. But we should respect the fact that something in the human mind, the musical mind, seems to demand the satisfaction of final restatement. In the same way that any three points in a three-dimensional space can be shown to be points on a circle, so a threefold musical structure tends to exhibit a cyclical order. The abstract truths of geometry have certain vital applications within the field of our musical experience. It all depends upon our ability to conceive primary geometrical relationships as relationships of thought emancipated from visual two-dimensional diagrams. The principles of musical structure can then immediately be grasped as specific applications of the first universal relationships of pure thought.

With such considerations in mind, it is instructive to contemplate one of the finest keyboard fantasias produced in the eighteenth century – Mozart K. 475 – which exhibits the cyclical order and contains heterogeneous material all with a considerable dramatic impact. Even such a bourgeois form as the Viennese waltz, which started its career as a stream of different tunes indifferently organized, eventually settled down with a developmental and recapitulatory coda. It is in the sonata-style, however, that this general principle appears to reach its most highly organized manifestations, and to this we must now turn.

Chapter six

C. P. E. Bach and the Sonata (1)

THE traditional view of Bach's place in musical history has always been reverential. For a long time it was thought that Emanuel was the virtual inventor of sonata-form, that Haydn (and Mozart to a lesser degree) took over his invention and brought it to the point where Beethoven could remould it according to his own grand designs. But we should note one thing straight away: the 'Prussian' sonatas, which were composed early in his life, already show a high degree of formal organization. Did this spring into being all at once? Does it not rather suggest a fairly long period of gestation and preliminary unfolding?[1] It is suggested that Bach did not invent the sonata-form at all, that his distinctive contribution to the history of the keyboard sonata lies less in the overall formal considerations and more in the kind and quality of the material which he associated with the sonata-principle generally and which, indeed, seemed already to have established itself as a convention when he began to compose sonatas. In other words, a point which is frequently made about Beethoven, namely that he adopted sonata-form and burst its traditional bonds by packing it with dynamic and subjectively impregnated material really applies to C. P. E. Bach. There is nothing revolutionary about the first movement of Beethoven's first pianoforte sonata – at any rate from the standpoint of form – which had not been anticipated in, say, the fourth 'Prussian' sonata of Bach.[2]

Let us, then, begin by making a clear distinction between a formal convention which is, after all, no more than a certain manner of arranging material, and something altogether different which ultimately absorbed the formal convention. The formal convention is the familiar pattern: Statement/Development/Restatement with which the textbooks have made us over-familiar. The something different is the new consciousness which we have already discussed in relation to the fantasia and the technique of improvisation, and which finds its outlet in diverse expressionism, contrast and variety. The convention has a perfectly respectable history and is quite at home with contrapuntal undramatic forms. It can be seen also in songs and dances. The new consciousness has at first no obvious connexions with it. It is concerned with psychological truth, with the ebb and flow of feeling, with variety, contrast and opposition. The interest of Bach's music is that it shows the two growing together. The Bach sonata is an alloy which demonstrates two contrary principles. First of all it shows us the natural inheritance of a traditional manner of tonal organization. Secondly, it shows us this traditional manner transmuted by a new psychological dynamic into something altogether revolutionary. We shall see that in one sense Bach has posed a big question to composer-theoreticians which has not yet been definitively answered: Is the sonata-principle an objective logical development, a matter of form alone, or is it the only finally satisfactory musical solution of the problem of unifying conflicting subjective impulses? What we call sonata-form is the bland, outward-looking face of something infinitely less neat. Its history is inseparably bound up with the successive attempts of composers to get to rational grips with their own subjective upsurge. The sonata-principle is the inner essence, the less-easily formulated dynamic which fuses and unifies and explores tensions. It is rather a principle of the imagination than the intellect. It seems like an expression of that 'esemplastic power' described by S. T. Coleridge in his distinction between Fancy and Imagination.[3] Coleridge conceived the imagination as a faculty which struggles to idealize and to unify images with a concern for some central conception which it is desired to convey. The imagination is thus the characteristic energy of the true poet, and a poem is more than a mere association of images. A good poem is a fusion of different elements within a form which is satisfying in its essential unity and directness of appeal. It orders our mental images with a dynamic oneness of purpose. Coleridge was very much influenced by German idealist philosophers, and it seems obvious to me that his theory of the imagination owes much to the philosophy of synthesis conceived by Hegel and Schelling. At any rate, such a conception has a special application to the sonata. The 'tonal imagery' which the composer works into a formal scheme must be integrated by an individual wholeness of conception. Many eighteenth-century sonata-form movements are composed of material which is fancifully associated rather than imaginatively fused by 'esemplastic power'. There is no vital antithesis, no impetus of organic impulse from phrase to phrase. Formally they are insipid. As the gravitational attraction of two rotating bodies balances the centrifugal out-thrust, and creates a tension which binds them irrevocably together, so the sonata-principle locks together tonal material presented in different keys. The principle of imaginative fusion is applied to tonal oppositions. It explores the vitality of antithesis and makes three out of two.

Generally speaking, what is usually called 'sonata-form' appeared quite early in the eighteenth century as the elaboration of simple binary form. Many dance-movements from J. S. Bach's English and French Suites, Partitas and so on, consist of two main sections divided by a double bar. The first section frequently shows a dual structure almost always associated with modulation to the dominant or a near-related key. The second section, after adventurous sallies of a developmental kind through more distant keys, returns to the tonic and restates the basic thematic idea. It is worth pointing out that the formal interest of such movements lies rather in the modulation scheme than in any pronounced element of thematic contrast. Frequently there is very little melodic contrast within the scope of a single movement, and the 'second theme', should there be one, often seems to be little more than some twist or turn from the main one taken over for extended treatment. Again, and especially in Bach and Handel, the texture is largely contrapuntal and any elements of thematic contrast are absorbed and integrated into a two or three or four-part web which reduces its significance.

For example, we may take the first movement of J. S. Bach's French Suite in B minor. This beautiful flowing movement in Bach's most characteristic keyboard style is virtually monothematic. It begins with the following running figure:

EX. 24

and after passing through the relative major modulates to the dominant minor simply by reiteration of the figure (a) at different levels:

EX. 25

The opening notes become increasingly significant as they are now divorced from their continuation. So far we see a single *motif* given contrasting tonal emphasis by the opposition of tonic and dominant.

Haydn is attached to the same procedure, and there is a clear case in the first movement of his Symphony in D, no. 104, where the same theme (differently harmonized) appears first in the tonic and then, after emphatic preparation for something apparently quite new, in the dominant.

In the second half of the movement, the opening figure (a) is immediately inverted; a long thread of melody takes the music through a number of keys, and analysis reveals that this thread consists entirely of a sequence of inverted statements of (a). Finally, with the return to the tonic key, (a) reappears in its original form. To the discerning ear this is really a very wonderful little movement. A threefold process of statement, development and return is clearly apparent despite close adherence to a melodic archetype.

The intense satisfaction derived from movements of this type is not easy to explain in words. Obviously, the human mind and spirit derive nourishment from such musical expressions of a threefold order. If this were not the case, tripartite forms would not feature so prominently in musical history. The main point is that this triple order is a matter of abstract relationships independent of precise elements of thematic contrast, and it tends to appear even in musical forms which seem to be characterized by a different numerical principle. We may pause to reflect that binary form seemed to generate the triple order out of its own being, so to speak, by a kind of spontaneous extension. The growth of musical consciousness is characterized at every phase of history by the tendency to state an idea, motive or theme and then elaborate it in some way.[4] Unelaborated melody usually belongs to a low order of civilization.[5] The mental, emotional or spiritual satisfaction which can be derived from the average popular song is very soon exhausted. The absence of an evolving formal dynamic necessarily places great emphasis upon rhythm alone, the first pulse of music which, in a very real sense, and as popular music reveals, leads straight back into the realm of unconscious impulse. Musical history, looked at from this point of view, is the record of the ascent of consciousness from depths of primitive apprehension which have their correlative in rhythm alone.

In the history of musical forms, the numerical principles of 2 and 3 are intertwined in various ways. If we call the Haydnesque Minuet and Trio ternary, we have still to recognize that the minuet and trio sections, separately considered, are frequently binary structures divided by a repeat, and that the second part of both minuet and trio generally extends in a developmental manner. In any case, the general procedure of starting in a tonic key, departing from it and extending what was first stated, and finally returning to it with some degree of restatement must always engender an abstract threefold relation. The issue cannot be forced; but triple relationship in music is so universal as to seem almost a necessary principle of tonal order. After all, the bare progression I-V-I is a threefold reciprocal relation with emotional overtones and virtually universal application.

Form, in this overall abstract sense, may not be unrelated to the basic harmonic concept of consonance-dissonance-consonance which is certainly a vital element in harmonic procedure. And this, in turn, is but the tonal expression of the psychological alternation of tension and release. Musical forms tend to grow, in a historical sense, by a process of internal generation. Greater and greater variety of internal organization is achieved in a single movement, whatever its original form-type, by the inward reflection of the overall, outer formal order into the parts, so that the parts become microcosmic epitomes, so to speak, of the whole. This observation will be seen to illuminate the sonatas of C. P. E. Bach. Let us first, however, measure it against the evolution of sonata-form.

Sonata-form grew from binary form by the following multiple process: first of all, binary form was extended by the increasingly developmental nature of the first part of the secondary statement. This increasing tendency to develop is the logical extension of the very tendency which brought binary form into being – namely, the experienced desire for a follow-on to a primary statement. Together with the developmental tendency, the first half of the binary structure began to bifurcate itself, firstly by increasing emphasis upon the tonic-dominant antithesis, secondly by the addition of thematic antithesis, which, however, is by no means so universal as commonly supposed. In the early days of sonata-form, that is in the first half of the eighteenth century, thematic antithesis is seldom powerful enough to generate a sense of violent emotional contrast. Contrapuntal textures tend to persist, and in so far as they do, tensions brought about by counterpoint overcome the rhythmic irregularities of contrasting thematic ideas. Thematic tension is smoothed out by simultaneous linear tension. It is a psychological fact that the most diverse thematic material can be rendered acceptable by sounding it simultaneously. Polytonality, for example, is essentially a linear device. Moreover, a contrapuntal texture, when highly organized, imposes a tremendous intellectual discipline upon what might otherwise be a predominantly emotional expression. Both in J. S. Bach's keyboard fugues and in Mozart's symphonies and quartets, an emotionally expressive melody is often sharply held in check by subjecting it to a contrapuntal discipline. When this discipline is abandoned, as it is frequently in Beethoven's early pianoforte sonatas, the resulting harmonic accompaniments – often constructed in block chords, arpeggios, spasms of Alberti bass and so on, produce a sense of rhythmic hiatus, and dislocate the emotional equilibrium. This has caused many writers and enthusiasts to speak of Beethoven's dramatic impulse, and his emotional expansion of the bounds of sonata-form, no doubt with a good deal of truth. The whole point about drama is that it dislocates some pre-existing equilibrium.

Except in one or two cases, notably Haydn's large-scale sonata in E flat[6] (composed for Mrs Bartolozzi) and Mozart's Sonata in C minor, K. 451, the more highly evolved sonata-form movements of Haydn and Mozart do not look forward to the explosive outbursts of Beethoven. What we seem to see are extended binary-form structures on a high plane of intellectual organization. These have been arrived at by a logical process of internal reflection, as described above. The development section is extended and intensified. The overall dual principle of the basic binary structure is applied to the first part of the movement, with distinction between tonic and dominant thematic groups. These groups then tend to become individualized, and frequently reveal their own internal binary organization. Then the concept of a bridge becomes increasingly important (its growing importance can be traced through Haydn's string quartets and symphonies) and the honest observer will be forced to confess that this is frequently also developmental in character – i.e. it extends an idea in the first statement and leads to a new key. There are thus three elements within the first section – first group (tonic key), bridge, and second group (dominant or relative major). After the development section, this threefold structure tends to return as restatement with, of course, appropriate modifications of key-relationship so that the music can end in the tonic. This general scheme can be observed in sonata-form movements in Haydn and Mozart, and in earlier symphonic movements by Stamitz and Monn, when there seems to be very little emphasis at all upon violent thematic contrast. Even when clearly distinguished themes are used in both first and second-subject groups in the exposition, they do not produce a sense of emotional upheaval or rhythmic dislocation. The unity within the overall variety is a unity achieved on the basis of the threefold order without the awareness of transcended subjective antitheses. Frequently, indeed, in the symphonies of the composers named, there is a prevailing suavity of mood, and the moments of greatest tension seem to be reserved for the development sections. The first and second subject groups, when they do contain thematic contrasts, generally embody an Italianate tunefulness which makes no intellectual and only the most superficial emotional demands. Haydn, indeed, frequently relies upon delightful gypsy-like tunes which are far removed from the traditional misconception of symphonic gravity. However, the very lightness of a great deal of symphonic material is deceiving. It is often a starting-point only – a happy link with the world of *opéra buffa* which stimulates a pleasant association-chain in the performer's or listener's aural memory. It often sparks off a great deal of intensely abstract symphonic thinking, for which the sonata-form convention provides a conveniently extended framework.

The development of C. P. E. Bach as a composer of sonatas reveals the gradual integration of factors which originally made quite separate appearances on the stage of musical history. Indeed, one might be excused for maintaining that this integration is never completely achieved. The awareness of the need to achieve it only seemed to grow upon him slowly, and for the greater part of his creative life, seemingly disparate elements coexist, often with a curiously incongruous effect. I think it is safe to say, and the point will be substantiated in the following analyses, that Bach did not, in his own mind, originally regard the evolving binary structure as an obvious vehicle for emotional expression of the kind which he exploited to the full in his fantasias. This statement is generally true of most keyboard composers who contributed to the establishment of the formal scheme we now know as sonata-form and then associate only with its later exponents. Domenico Scarlatti is full of emotional vitality and lively melody. Cimarosa wrote some effervescent sonata-form movements likewise full of froth and bubble and engaging tunefulness. Antonio Soler carried on the tradition of the one-movement sonata in extended binary form, and even used dramatic contrasts of key in his exposition – though these are more dramatic in visual notation than in tonal effect. The sonatas of these composers are characterized by what Stravinsky once called the principle of sameness rather than the principle of difference. Sameness is the legacy of baroque, and is a quality of music existing on a basis of 'ontological time'. J. S. Bach is perhaps the greatest exemplar, and he had many contemporaries whose work shows the same feature. Difference is the mark of music which dislocates the natural objective pulse of things, and substitutes a subjective experience of temporal relationships which is relative to it. Beethoven is the most obvious case – early and middle-period Beethoven at any rate. Stravinsky's way of putting this is somewhat mystical; but it is not difficult to grasp his point.

What marks out C. P. E. Bach from his contemporaries[7] and forerunners is his frank acceptance of the principle of difference, the substitution of a subjective scheme of temporal relationships for the accepted flow of the natural pulse as it seems to be embodied in baroque music. There is an analogy with the position reached in the world of drama. If the classical world of the three unities, represented especially by Corneille, was overthrown by Hugo in the name of the romantic principle, so the unity of mood associated with baroque instrumental movements was broken up by stabs of contrasting feeling, halting rhythms, enharmonic modulations and all the devices of *Empfindsamkeit*.

Having accepted the principle of difference, which is, after all, only a more metaphysical way of defining the aesthetic of *Empfindsamkeit*, it was some time before Emanuel Bach applied it wholeheartedly to the sonata-form framework which he embraced without reservations in his 'Prussian' sonatas.

The sonata as a whole was conceived by Bach and his Berlin contemporaries as a threefold structure. In many of his sonatas, especially the earlier ones, a sense of overall integration is lacking. Movements seem to be associated in an almost haphazard manner. There are considerable stylistic differences between them, and one feels that irreconcilable elements are being forced into an unconvincing association. It is not unusual to find a rather 'stringy' first movement made up of tenuous, rambling melodic lines in two parts, followed by an extremely romantic adagio characterized by a more satisfying harmonic texture, and rounded off by an inconsequential rococo finale. (In this general prescription he was closely followed by Georg Benda.) The fifth sonata in the *Versuch* examples is of this type. The sense of syncretism is particularly strong here because the first movement is in E flat, the second in B flat minor, and the last in F major. The fact that these movements are related on a basis of stepwise fifths does not really overcome it. Generally speaking, however, the order of keys is what we would consider conventional. In the later sonatas, and this is a significant point, the sense of internal integration within the sonata-form movements is extended to the sonata as a whole. The principle of unity in variety which emerges in the complete, three-movement composition is reflected in the composition of the individual movements, and especially in the first movements.

In Bach's sonatas we can study the emergence of a system of tonal logic which is still the basis of serious musical composition in the larger forms. It applies both to parts and wholes, and underpins the relation between them. This logic seems to be the synthesis of two principles, an inherited objective order and a subjective dynamic which demanded tension between opposing factors – between keys, themes, sections and whole movements. Bach's achievement was his intellectual grasp of the synthesis which seemed to him to be implied by the musical situation of his day, and by his own ambition to make music a flexible means of conveying feeling and passion. As a theorist and experimentalist – even as a kind of tonal alchemist – he must have been aware of the formal pull of the extended binary concept on the one hand, and the anarchical tendency of uninhibited expressiveness on the other. We have already examined the methods whereby he achieved his ideal of musical expression. We will now analyze the way in which he fused the inwardness of his musical inspiration with the formal vehicle which he adopted in his sonatas. Obviously, the methods of a composer like Kuhnau were not adequate for his purposes. Emotionally, he must have been out of tune with them.

Kuhnau's sonatas are essentially baroque in conception, and unmistakably affirm the principle of sameness. True, they contain movements contrasted in tempo and key-relationship; but they are very strongly bound by the contrapuntal discipline of the baroque era, and are closer to the suite than the threefold unity which Bach seemed to have in mind. Moreover, the individual sections in Kuhnau's sonatas are largely dominated by a single idea.

Chapter seven

C. P. E. Bach and the Sonata (2)
The 'Prussian' Sonatas

THE first movement of the first 'Prussian' sonata has a number of interesting features which show its kinship with earlier styles. It begins with a simple figure which is immediately imitated in the bass. The imitation serves as a bass for the continuation of the treble-line:

EX. 26

This is immediately followed by a capriccio type of figure in D minor also imitated in the bass, but this time in C major:

EX. 27

A modulating passage, which confirms the texture firmly in the dominant key is then cancelled out by a kind of second subject which begins in C minor, again modulates, and finally comes to a cadence in C major. This passage makes use of part of EX. 27:

EX. 28

Figure (a) of EX. 26 is then reintroduced as an embryonic stretto, the treble opening leading to a high dominant pedal note which creates a sense of climax. (If this had come from an oratorio one would expect trumpets here!) The texture becomes a three-part web and suddenly collapses on to a bare octave:

EX. 29

Three points may be made at once. Thus far the music has more than a mild flavour of the concerto grosso about it – heightened by the marked contrast between the quiet EX. 28 and the forte ending in three parts. Secondly, most of the thematic presentation occurs in two parts only. Thirdly, the generally contrapuntal layout of the material tends to mask the variety of melodic figuration which this short section contains.

The second part of the movement contains a clear development section beginning with an inversion of the main theme and answered by its original form. This leads into an extended sequence on the basis of the inverted figure, and eventually to a restatement of the three-part climax, including the dominant pedal note, which leads straight into chromatic elaboration and a cadence in D minor:

EX. 30

(climax of development in 3 parts)

The restatement is not simply a literal presentation of the opening material with appropriate modifications of key. The opening figure leads into a free passage in two parts, and the transition to the 'second subject' is made without the appearance of EX. 27. The movement ends with the forte in three parts, and then collapses on to the bare final.

The second movement, deservedly well-known, and quoted in anthologies and analytical texts, is a dramatic surprise after the first. It consists of alternate arioso and recitative passages. The recitative is highly effective, yet is little more than a keyboard transcription of a familiar vocal manner. Even so, it marks a new phase in the history of the sonata. One does not have to look far in order to see its direct connexion with the rhapsodic manner of the fantasias. In quest of dramatic expression, Bach introduces the most daring modulations:

EX. 31

After this movement, the finale is again a surprise, since it reverts at once to the jig style which is prominent in the last movement of keyboard suites. It contains three clear melodic motives, the first one receiving development in the second half at the expense of the second, which is never heard again. The first figure contains a sound (bracketed) which occurs frequently in Emanuel Bach's melodies, and which is something of a mannerism. The third is perhaps more properly regarded as a consequent of the second. It contributes vitality to the movement by a series of sequential downward and upward-resolving appogiaturas:

EX. 32

EXX. 33a, b, c

The second sonata shows a higher degree of integration, taking the three movements as a whole, than the preceding one. This is because the first movement advances farther towards the aesthetic standpoint of the second which, in these earlier works, is usually the vehicle of Bach's more enduring thoughts. The first movement is untroubled by naïve contrapuntal devices, and it contains some interesting and varied figuration. The first theme is self-contained, and begins with a triplet run which does not recur until the closing group of the exposition. More interesting is the immediate presentation of a contrasting theme after the opening flourish, and the subsequent raising of tension by a sequence characterized by rising appogiaturas:

EXX. 34a, b

The closing group, in its turn, makes an abrupt break with its antecedent material, and exploits the enharmonic antithesis of major and minor, coming to a half-close on a dominant seventh in C. The natural B is then brusquely dismissed by the closing triplets.

It seems obvious that performance on a modern pianoforte with the strict adherence to tempo which would normally apply to a sonata by Mozart or Clementi will not do at all for a movement like this. It requires the tone and 'key-feel' of the clavichord, and a sensitive rubato. One would wish the runs in the sequential passages to be somewhat 'crushed', and the appogiaturas at the end of the runs to be slightly dragged. There would also have to be a subtle interpretation of the turns and trills, and a readiness to exploit every possiblity of light and shade, in order that the inherent expressiveness of this little movement should be revealed in full.

It is also obvious that movements of this type had a considerable influence upon Josef Haydn, whose sonata-form structures show just the same contrast of thematic ideas, tonality and rhythmic devices. Most characteristic of Haydn is the sudden opposition between running scale-wise passages and homophonic structures built up on a constant metrical pulse:

EXX. 35a, b

The slow movement has a lingering baroque quality which lends it strength. It consists of a long train of ruminative melody sparked off by a broken and melancholy phrase which offers opportunities for passionate declamation and alternate forte and piano:

EX. 36

As the movement evolves, various possibilities of chromatic melody are employed to superb effect:

EX. 37

the texture being occasionally punctuated by plangent chords stabbed out
in dotted rhythm. This fine movement seems to combine the baroque
soliloquizing characteristic of both J. S. Bach and Vivaldi with the
dramatic flourishes of an operatic lament. Aesthetically speaking, it has
much in common with the adagio in the last sonata of the 'Prussian' set,
which has a similar opening phrase and the same kind of alternate arioso
and recitative:

EX. 38

Clementi has written movements in a very similar vein. The following
example comes from his Sonata in F sharp minor Opus 26 No 2:

EX. 39

The finale of the second 'Prussian' sonata is vivacious and full of
melodic ideas. It is characteristic of the way Bach organizes his time-
space: four lines of music comprehend a rhythmic and tonal variety
which it is staggering to compare with the often febrile tunefulness of his
contemporaries.

The third sonata has a Scarlatti-like quality in the opening allegro and
in the finale. The melodic material of the first movement is undistin-
guished; but it serves as a vehicle for a roving modulatory scheme. The
first theme, for example, is stated completely in E major. It is immediately
extended by a transitional passage commencing in E minor, and modulating through G major, A minor/major and B minor/major. Ambiguity
between major and minor is common in Bach's music, and is frequently
achieved, as here, by the combined use of flat sixths and major thirds:

EX. 40

The remainder of the exposition is simply a sequential run first under and then over an ornamented pedal (a device common to J. S. Bach) and a broken passage in the manner of D. Scarlatti. The finale opens, like the first movement, with a self-contained eight-bar phrase. It looks forward to a Haydn sonata in the same key with respect to its pauses and the 'huntsman' chords which bring it to a close:

EXX. 41a, b

The development section of this finale has a very organic quality, and the recapitulation of the opening theme is varied.

The middle movement of the sonata looks backward in spirit to the beautiful prelude-style of J. S. Bach; but its flowing three-part lyricism nevertheless has something new to contribute. Without any prejudice to the traditional concept of J. S. Bach counterpoint, it manages to introduce sighs and expressive appogiaturas of melting expressiveness and almost feminine wistfulness. Note also the thematic connection at (a):

EXX. 42a, b

Another passage looks back to the Fugue in D major (WTC II) by J. S. Bach, and at the same time anticipates the richness of the harmony of later times:

K.M.B.–F

EXX. 43a, b

Altogether, this is one of Emanuel's most beautiful movements, and reveals a facet of his musical mentality which is not often dwelt upon by other commentators. In contributing something uniquely his own, he yet seems to bring together the 'book-ends' between which the classical style is nurtured. This unique contribution shows how one style can slowly yield to another, and how the transitional product can yet exhibit an intrinsic beauty which elevates it above its transitional function. Again, we have a fine example of Emanuel Bach's musical thinking. He had an integrative mind which was perpetually bent upon the unification of different elements. It is as much revealed in a movement of this type as in the sonatas taken as a whole, or in the sonata-form first movements.

Turning to the fourth sonata, we sense that something like a formula for first movements is crystallizing in Bach's mind. The opening allegro starts with a theme which has a strong family likeness to the opening flourish of J. S. Bach's C minor fantasia. By now, indeed, the tendency towards the use of opening themes derived from the notes of the common chord after the Mannheim pattern is well established, and it was to serve composers of sonatas and symphonies for at least another century. A further, and more subtle yet closely connected tendency is also emerging. The extent to which the opening theme, in so far as it is an extension of the tonic triad, remains close in thematic structure to the notes of that triad, frequently offers a clue to the complexity of the movement it introduces.

Modern thought has made us familiar with the idea that the existence of physical matter – that is spatial structure – depends upon a pattern of relationships maintained in time. For music a similar principle is true, although for space we must substitute the medium of tone, which is to a musical structure as physical space is to a three-dimensional form. Moreover, we must bear in mind that the dimensional quality of 'tonal space' depends upon the quality of subjective experience informing it. Whether a composition is extended or compressed, whether it is contrapuntal or homophonic, whether it is simple or complex in key-structure – all these factors depend upon the quality of the creative consciousness. For instance, there is a real sense in which we can say, using the analogy of distance, that C major and G major are relatively close together, whereas C major and C sharp minor are relatively farther apart. In 1780, a composer writing a C major sonata tended repeatedly to present secondary material in G major. In 1880 he invariably sought greater key-contrast, even in a short composition. The explanation for this cannot be found or offered simply on the basis of an objective analysis of musical structures and techniques. These very structures and techniques are expressions of qualities of consciousness. The move from C/G major to C/C sharp minor reveals a fundamental change in the quality of human experience. The tonal space of music is the ever-fluctuating objective mode of a plastic, subjective, ever-variable musical energizing which permeates it. That is why the most abstract and seemingly 'intellectual' structures of J. S. Bach can yet reveal a profoundly affecting subjective apprehension.

When a melody is derived from a single chord, we have a temporal extension of a simultaneity – the chord is the tonal space of the melody, so to speak, and the melody is the time of the chord.[1] Here is an interesting example from WTC II:

EX. 44

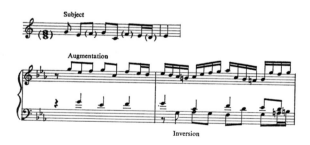

Such matters open up fascinating fields of speculation which are beyond the scope of this work. However, it is worth lingering here for a moment. The mere analysis of interesting musical facts without attempting any principle of explanation is unrewarding – indeed, it could be regarded as an abdication from the responsibility to meet the metaphysical challenge music constantly presents to us.

In relation to the temporal spread of a theme, a chord which substantiates it is ideally a timeless entity. A chord is an ideal construction, a once-for-all subsumption of the musico-geometric relations which have virtually infinite possibilities of permutation in temporal extension.[2] In this sense, harmony is to space as melody is to time; and in so far as the equations of Einstein demand the integral and comprehensive concept of space-time, so any adequate critique of music demands an analogous concept which recognizes the integrality and comprehensiveness of the 'vertical' and 'horizontal' elements of music. Schönberg tried to establish just such a concept in his theory of tone-rows. Whether we think in terms of twelve chromatic tones, or more traditionally, it is quite true that the creative musician tends to work from a matrix which is, in fact, a kind of 'space-time nucleus'. Bearing in mind that in music space 'condenses to a point' (Hegel),[3] and that this point is tone, the musician is all the time involved, subjectively by feeling, objectively by thought, in the un- ravelling of the temporal possibilities of certain complexes of sound which are in fact epitomes of abstract spatial relations. These epitomes are really microcosms of design. Rudolph Reti was fascinated with this way of regarding music, and his book *The Thematic Process in Music* is really a book of analyses grounded in a similar metaphysical position.

It frequently happens that the more obvious, both to the ear and to the mind, is the presence of a 'vertical' at the outset of an abstract composition like a sonata or a fugue, the greater the intellectual depth required to work out its possibilities. The more a work begins with thematic material grounded in a recognizable chord (generally a tonic) the more complex is the organization of tonal space invited by such material. It does not always happen. There are many shallow and superficial sonata- movements in the eighteenth century which seem little more than noise and fury running between tonic and dominant chords. But the general tendency is there. The common chord is frequently the beginning of a complex skein and has the same relation to the movement growing out of it as the first tones of the harmonic series have to Western music as a whole. The ultimate development is found in those romantic symphonies which begin with a slowly articulated shimmering chord. They generally take a long time to play. Beethoven's ninth and Bruckner's fourth sym- phonies are cases in point.

Harmonic melodies are generally expansive, and, to use an apt word, spacious. They also tend to generate 'fragmentation' forms more than melodies based on scalic series. Such forms are built up out of contrasting harmonic fragments which are unified by the underlying universality of the basic harmonic relations and the very tension generated by the different rhythmic periods. One wonders whether the overall expansion which the development of sonata-form brought to the musical scene is related to this fact. Given a first subject in the tonic and a second in the dominant, we have immediately two subjects related by the defining polarities of the tonic chord. This is a larger phase of the linear spread of a vertical relation. When a work contains much material extended from common chords, then the stage is set for an expansive 'fragmentation' form, and much developmental work. A fine example is Mozart's keyboard sonata in C minor, K. 457.[4]

In the first movement of Bach's fourth 'Prussian' sonata, we find more highly organized musical thinking than anywhere else in this set, and, as previously suggested, the movement foreshadows a general tendency in the subsequent history of the classical sonata. The first theme opens with an arpeggio of the tonic chord in C minor, and apart from an appogiatura on the dominant, it remains on or around the tonic notes:

EX. 45

An interesting transition to the dominant follows immediately, and this yields, after a pause, to a yearning phrase in F minor:

EX. 46

which, as the example shows, is a varied reprise of the first subject. These rising triplets are a mannerism and are to be found throughout the entire range of Bach's keyboard music. The ensuing phrase is again a familiar pattern (see EXX. 38 and 42b), derived from the opening:

EX. 47

and leads to a nostalgic melody in E flat. Parts of this have an affinity with the arpeggiated tonic chord with which the movement begins:

EX. 48

The modulating sevenths which climb to the half-close in E flat are similar to those in the middle of the 'Hamlet' Fantasia:

EXX. 49a, b

The *Empfindsamkeit* of this passage is immediately translated into the idiom of D. Scarlatti:

EX. 50

This introduces a new theme containing subsidiary *Affekte*. I quote the latter part of it, which begins with a repetition of its opening phrase an octave lower, and incorporates a D flat – a very heartfelt moment. The third statement of the phrase X leads straight into a rapid triplet passage which, right at the end, echoes the rising triplets in the opening theme, before dropping to a cadence in E flat:

EX. 51

Those who regard Emanuel Bach as the father of the sonata should examine this exposition carefully. Its most significant characteristic is not a clearly definable first subject, bridge-passage, second subject scheme. From that abstract standpoint these bars are extremely difficult to analyse; and even if we do force the material into such an arbitrary tripartite scheme, it is immediately obvious that this does less than justice to what we hear. But this exposition is nevertheless a fine demonstration of the sonata-principle. The emotional range is tremendous, and this finds its necessary complement in the modulation scheme. Let us see what the composer does with all this material.

Study of the second half of the movement shows that development and recapitulation are fused in an interesting way. Development begins at once with a statement of the opening theme in the relevant major key of E flat; but this leads quickly into sequential passage-work through the tonic to a half-close in G minor. Without any further preliminary, Bach reintroduces EX. 47 and its follow-up material, EXX. 48 and 49. Having reached the half-close again in G minor, Bach suddenly unleashes a brusque and angry burst of arpeggiation which introduces a brief reference to EX. 51 and a strange modulation, before coming to a full close in the dominant minor:

EX. 52

The opening theme is now stated again, and this time its sequential extension takes the music back to the tonic minor. When this reaches the dominant chord, the affecting strains of EX. 51 are heard for the last time, and the movement ends with the same figuration as that concluding the exposition.

There are different ways of accounting for the structure of this varied and interesting movement. If we accept that the main thematic material is contained in EXX. 45, 47 and 51, which we can symbolize A, B and C respectively, then the whole movement reveals the following pattern (omitting subsidiary features already described):

A	C minor	
B	E flat major	Exposition
C	E flat major	

A	E flat major	
B	G minor	Development and
A	G minor – C minor	recapitulation fused
C	C minor	

For reasons which will be discussed in a moment, we can also symbolize the movement like this:

$$C$$

$$E\flat \qquad G$$

If we regard B as the real 'second subject' and C as a farewell phrase or closing group, then the position of B in the development/recapitulation appears somewhat ambiguous. We can say that Bach presents his second subject before the first when recapitulating the main material. (Clementi was attached to this kind of formal inversion.) On the other hand, if the recapitulation proper begins only with the final appearance of the main theme in G minor, then the development can be said to contain full statements of first and second subjects. The formal recapitulation can then be regarded as abbreviated in order to preserve balance.

But we can, if we please, regard C as the real second subject, and B as intermediary material. The recapitulation can then be said to concern itself with essentials – simple statements of the two main subjects.

Yet is not this one of those innumerable cases where the textbook analytical scheme is inapplicable to the concrete reality of the music? I use the word 'concrete' here in its full philosophical signification. Music can only exist 'concretely' in actual experience. Its existence in the mind of an analyst is an astral parody compared with its sounding reality in the tonal imagination, under the hands, and in the ears of a performer. The moment we pay attention to the concrete reality of the music, it becomes immediately apparent that the verbal juggling necessitated by the academic desire to categorize musical tissue according to set schemes of thought does violence to experience. Is there a form of words which does not do violence to experience?

This movement is a highly organized unity. It is also a variety. The variety of thematic and tonal relationships appears to be the direct outward expression of a fluctuating emotional impulse – a stream of *Affekte* expressing a single basic creative urge. The critical understanding of a musical unity-in-variety depends upon the extent to which we can grasp this principle: that the flow of consciousness is continuous – an apparent tautology which underlines what we often forget. Variations of emotional ebb and flow take place within this continuous consciousness. It is in virtue of the ebb and flow of change that the continuum is in fact subjectively aware. The tonal variety which is exhibited in the contrasting rhythms, melodies and key-relationships is a direct objective revelation of the emotional ebb and flow, which, because it manifests in a continuum, is therefore also manifesting an underlying unity. The aesthetic unity which permeates the tonal variety of a sonata-form movement is the objective 'transposition' of the primary, subjective unity which bestows coherence upon the phenomena of consciousness. The integration of key-relationship sensed throughout a movement which nevertheless contains many modulations is a symbolic acknowledgement of this primary unity.

Three general phases within the movement analysed above can indeed be determined quite clearly. Difficulties begin when we endeavour to be too precise, or to force every tonal event within the movement into conformity with the Procrustean scheme of the textbooks. There is a phase which expounds material; there is a phase which is developmental; there is a phase which is recapitulatory. In this movement developmental and recapitulatory procedures are fused.

Such an approach to analysis is in closer conformity with experience, which has no sharp edges. Events interpenetrate one another, and two disparate events can yet, in retrospect, seem to illuminate one another. This is not unreasonable, because in so far as they take place within the same continuum of consciousness they are, in some sense, relational. Consciousness, moreover, becomes more integrated, more purposive and more dynamic, the more it relates, assimilates and orders its phenomena, and the less it resembles a dripping tap through which valuable experiences fall upon the waste land of meaninglessness and fatuity.

These reflections are not irrelevant to any real understanding of the history of the sonata-principle. Every art-historian pays lip-service to 'environment'. But it is not enough to pick upon the more obvious features of the contemporary social scene. The immediate environment of a work of art is the consciousness within which it is born. That consciousness lives in certain vital relationships with the thought and the collective experience of its time. In so far as any common principles underlying that thought and experience can be determined, we have to be aware of them and state them clearly. In so far as these vital relationships are unconscious, we have to give them at least a speculative definition.

Having given these philosophical points their due, we can now contemplate an interesting fact about the movement we are considering. The three general phases of the entire movement, which is in C minor, are

respectively correlated with the three notes of the tonic chord – C, E flat
and G, tonic, mediant and dominant. Bearing in mind what was said
earlier about the linear extension of 'harmonic space', it is tempting to
regard the whole movement, paying due tribute to Schenker, as a 'prolongation' of the chord of C minor. Indeed, the devotees of monotonality
would regard this movement as a magnificent justification of their principle. I suggest that it is more to the point to consider how the chord of
C minor, considered as an 'epitome of abstract relations', or a microcosm
of design, has brought into being a lengthy and complex movement, and
how the layout of the three phases in three keys is a larger expression of the
basic relationships which are expressed in the first few notes of the opening
theme. The three main keys involved (C minor, E flat major and G
minor) are related to one another within a 'triangular' scheme. It is also
an interesting point that the numerical division of the monochord which
produces the perfect fifth is 3. When applied to the circle, and not to the
monochord which is, so to speak, a straight line, this number produces
triangularity. 'Sacred proportions' were known to the cathedral builders
who elaborated complex designs on the basis of geometrical figures which
served as symbols to the religious consciousness. It is quite possible that
they were also aware of the musical intervals corresponding to the simple
geometrical figures. But it is fascinating to study the growth of a musical
and formal principle which returns again, though doubtless unconsciously,
to this primary basis. In the case of Emanuel Bach, the quest is subjective
expression; but it would seem that the best tonal medium for such
expression has to come to terms with the universal principles which
underlie all design in any physical medium.[5]

On the other hand, we have to ask whether this movement shows Bach
moving towards the ever clearer definition of the threefold principle of
sonata-form, or whether we see him deliberately modifying an already
accepted formal scheme. In actual fact, the liberal way of laying out
material characteristic of the work just analysed has its close parallels in
the symphonic writing of the nineteenth century. Mahler's first movements often show a similar scheme. Mahler, moreover, is consciously
seeking to establish, as a formal musical principle, the concept of a
symphony being a 'world' of experience. Is Bach, and with due allowance
for his historical position, coloured by much the same ideal? It would not
be unreasonable to suppose that he took over the threefold order, conceived his sonata-form movements as 'little worlds' of feeling and expression, and did not hesitate to modify the abstract form in accordance
with his individual subjective requirements.

Whatever the truth of the matter, it is undeniable that this sonata is
indeed a little world. The heartfelt adagio is full of beautiful things, the
restlessness of the first movement having now yielded to a yearning

lyricism enhanced with melting cadences and appogiaturas. It is perhaps worth noting that the following phrase has thematic connexions with EX. 48 in the first movement:

EX. 53

The finale returns to the concerto grosso idiom. It is characterized by fluid running passages, and snatches of imitation which are not rigorously developed. There is also some decorative work reminiscent of violin figuration.

The fifth sonata is a neat essay in what might be called a 'heightened' *galante* style – i.e. *stile galante* endowed with a richer expressiveness than the term usually implies. The first movement is essentially a minuet and there is a fair amount of plain melody accompanied by repeated crotchets and spiced with occasional chromaticism. The repeated notes would not, especially in this rhythm, have been unobjectionable to ears attuned to the steady three-in-a-bar tempo of the ballroom minuet; but they sound a little dull to modern performers. The movement is also marred by stock cadence-figures; but then, again, a modern ear is somewhat spoiled by over-familiarity with the beautiful way Mozart handled the perfect cadence. Even so, such figures as the following are hall-marks of Emanuel's style, and we should grant him these marks of originality:

EXX. 54a, b, c

The andante is a lyrical stream broken only by expressive pauses. Some phrases have the sweetness of early classicism. In the following example, the prolonged dominant pedal bestows a throbbing bass which Bach, on his clavichord, would have exploited to good effect:

EX. 55

The finale abounds in efficient C major figuration, and at its best looks forward to similar movements in Mozart's pianoforte sonatas.

The last sonata is an altogether more powerful composition, and consists of a dramatic adagio sandwiched between two highly intellectual allegro movements. The first movement opens quietly enough, and then explodes in an ebullient spread of triplets which are only occasionally halted by more melodic material:

EX. 56

Two elements in the adagio appear to be related to similar things in the development section of the first movement, and hint at an integral structural motive binding the two together. The development, varying the opening flourish, begins like this:

EX. 57

Four lines farther on we find this:

EX. 58

The adagio opens with this phrase:

EX. 38

and leads on to:

EX. 59

The interplay of these contrasting ideas produces a fine movement. This vein has also been worked over by Clementi. His F sharp minor sonata referred to elsewhere has a first and second movement aesthetically akin to these.

The finale concedes little to mere tunefulness, and deals exhaustively with a figure which appears first in two-part counterpoint. In this it resembles many a symphonic finale by Haydn which begins in similar manner and in no time at all plunges vigorously into an intense contrapuntal *tour de force*:

EXX. 60a, b

It is not necessary, and it would not be fitting to analyse the 'Prussian' sonatas in greater detail. Enough has been said to show that these works not only define the broad outlines of the classical sonata but also give the sonata-principle an original and arresting expression.

In the first movements we can sense a permeating and dynamic feeling for unity in variety. In sonatas 4 and 6, at least, Bach has composed fine music in every movement, and has produced works displaying a high degree of overall integration. The tripartite form is clearly apparent in the first movements, and frequently also in the finales. In the fourth sonata, especially, the three-part scheme of the first movement is magnificently integrated with the vital and varied tonal material of which it is composed. This bringing together of the abstract concept and the concrete content is, I suggest, the hall-mark of the sonata-principle generally, and the main contribution of C. P. E. Bach to its history. In the 'Prussian' sonatas, Bach takes the abstract concept and attempts to fuse it, with considerable success in the case of the fourth sonata, with his own vein of creative expressiveness – that same dynamic subjectivity which he rationalized in his theory of improvisation.

We shall now consider subsequent phases of this blending of abstract and concrete in his later sonatas.

Chapter eight

C. P. E. Bach and the Sonata (3)
The 'Württemberg' Sonatas

THESE sonatas were composed very shortly after the 'Prussian' set. Although it would seem unreasonable to look for striking advances in style and technique, the fact remains that they are generally longer and frequently more daring in the exploitation of contrast. If we accept that the 'Prussian' sonatas have a great many experimental features, I think we can go on to suppose that having successfully launched one experimental set, Bach gained more confidence, and pushed the boundaries of his musical imagination a little farther. One result of this expansion of horizons is a general tendency towards ebullient outbursts, frequently of a quite unusual kind. This is especially true of the third sonata in the set, which begins, metaphorically speaking, with outstretched arms.

At the same time, taking the sonatas as a whole, there is an increasing sense of homogeneity. These works hang together better. The three-movement pattern has discovered its own principle of coherence, so to speak; one can enjoy the wholeness of the thing during performance. In the light of the subsequent history of the sonata-style, these compositions are very revealing. If, by some chance, the later classical composers had never lived – if music had somehow by-passed classical Vienna and evolved directly into the lyrical rhapsodies of the romantic era – one would still marvel at Bach's grasp of a high principle of tonal order, and the skill with which he fused conflicting elements by the fire of imagination and the discipline of intellect. Of course, to the creative mind, imagination and intellect are but the two sides of a single coin. The imagination, rightly considered, never violates the highest insights of reason. Indeed, it frequently vindicates and illuminates the pathways of reason. One wonders what went on in the minds of all those anonymous clavichordists, men, perhaps of culture and insight, who bought their copies of the 'Württemberg' sonatas, and who, playing them alone in the privacy of their quiet apartments, were led to ponder the impact of this new and vigorous art. Did they like 'this modern stuff' or find it distasteful to the ear? Did they keep their elegant minds open in the *salons*; but privately wonder where music was going? Or did they have the kind of experience so aptly described by Edward Caird in a monumental essay on *Goethe and Philosophy*:[1]

> 'Creative imagination is a power which is neither lawless, nor yet, strictly speaking, under law; it is a power which . . . makes laws. It carries us with free steps into a region in which we leave behind and forget the laws of nature; yet as soon as we begin to look round us and to reflect on our new environment, we see that it could not have been otherwise. The World has not been turned upside down, but widened by the addition of a new province which is in perfect continuity with it.'

Earlier (Chapter four), we discussed the aesthetic of C. P. E. Bach in respect of the idea that art is the imitation of nature, and examined the cult of *Empfindsamkeit* in some detail. In Bach's music, it is unquestionably true that the indwelling dynamic is nothing less than the forging of music from feeling, emotion and passion; and these three are, so to speak, the *prima materia* of the natural man. Now that we have examined some aspects of Bach's thought in the sonata-idiom, it will be profitable to consider this point a little further in the light of another, and most illuminating passage by Edward Caird.[2]

Caird points out that Goethe, like so many poets and musicians, also had his *Sturm und Drang* period, and that this ended with *Werther*. Then began:

> '. . . a movement towards limit and measure, which culminated at the end of his Italian journey. If in this new phase of thought nature was still worshipped, it was no longer regarded as a power that reveals itself at once in the immediate appearances of the outward world, or in the immediate impulses of the human spirit. It was now the *natura naturans* of Spinoza – i.e. as Goethe conceived it, a plastic organizing force which works secretly in the outward and especially in the organic world, and which in human life reveals itself most fully as the ideal principle of art. Clinging, as an artist, to the external, Goethe now sees that the truth of nature does not lie immediately on the surface, but in a unity which can be grasped only by a penetrative insight. Demanding, as a poet, that the ideal should not be separated from the sensuous, he is now conscious that the poetic truth of the passions shows itself, not in their immediate expression, *but only when their conflict leads to their "purification", and so reveals a higher principle.*'

The italics in the last sentence are mine: *Conflict – Purification – Higher Principle*. Here is the kernel of a vital insight which permeates not only the work of Goethe, but also the music of the Viennese masters, and which makes its first dramatic musical appearance in the compositions of Emanuel Bach. What seems so obvious to the inner eye of the mind which meditates deeply about the new creative force manifesting itself in the latter half of the eighteenth century is that art, and music in particular, show a swift ascent in the collective consciousness of man from the basic stuff of a vigorous and tingling experience to the ultimate categorical assertion of the principle of unity. But in music, of course, this is unity sensuously apprehended in the first instance. Nevertheless, the final experience builds a bridge between the sensuous and the ideal. The classical sonata, at its finest, reveals the fusion of passion and principle, of the particular subjective *Affekt* and the universal order. It is because, in music, the subjective particular was so genuine, so much stressed, that the rise of the sonata-principle was able to take place without serious risk of ambush by the wearisome dragon of purely abstract intellectualism and formal mechanics. It is certainly true that this particular dragon claimed its victims. Some of Emanuel Bach's contemporaries, G. Benda for instance, wrote keyboard sonatas which imitate the formal devices of Bach but often fail to enshrine any really interesting or stirring content. There are parallels in our own day. It is especially interesting that the ultra-expressiveness of the late nineteenth century led first to the tonal swamp of early Schönberg, and subsequently to serialism. Here again we see a familiar tendency repeating itself, though in this case the 'plastic, organizing force', having arrived at dodecaphony, quickly solidified into an intellectual cult from which, in our own day, it is struggling to extricate itself. But the triumph of the new principle over dry formalism and intellectual abstraction was never really in question, as it is perhaps not long delayed in our own day. Inspired by Emanuel Bach's clavichord sonatas, Josef Haydn subsequently devoted the greater part of his life to the consolidation of the sonata-principle.

The difference between the sonata-principle and the abstract concept of sonata-form is the difference between organism and mechanism. Sheer mechanism in music produces only stillborn offspring. Organism in the world of nature and art alike can only grow and enrich itself when it is informed by the principle of unity. And this unity can only enter the dwelling-house of the subjective consciousness when the *prima materia* of passion is purified. This form of words may sound mystical and hieratic, but it bears upon the crux of the sonata-principle precisely at the point where subjective feeling is disciplined by, and passes over into objective form, and where the objective designs of the abstract intellect acknowledge and yield to the positive dynamic of experience. The subjective

K.M.B.–G

tensions are the ground and vindication of the form; and the form, in its aesthetic quality, is considered in abstraction only at the cost of that which brought it into being, that which makes it live, and without which it is nothing more than a jangle of notes.

At the present time we are still caught up in the fashion for detailed structural analysis. This is a fascinating pursuit; but it testifies to the present one-sidedness of our musical consciousness. Whilst our abstract intellects, detached from any sense of subjective involvement, are dissecting music continuously in the fashionable quarterlies, both performers and composers are tending to respond to this carving-up of the tissue of musical experience by producing a very great deal of colourless, quasi-musical clatter – justified, of course, by some anti-musical and certainly anti-subjective theory. It is permissible to dredge the unconscious mind, apparently. It is not permitted to many to perceive the predetermined unity of organic form and the higher reaches of human experience. There is a direct connexion between the spirituality of a motet by Josquin and its musical form, a sonata-movement by Beethoven and the living fire of his initial inspiration. This connexion is immediately obvious to an integrated mind unhampered by the pressure which the contemporary intellectual *cultus* tries to apply to every worth-while musical experience.

A famous Oriental scholar has asserted that the truth of the subject is eternally enshrined in the object, and the truth of the object is likewise contained in the subject. This *aperçu* should be upheld by all those who are content to allow the sensuous impact of music to sit loose to its indwelling formal relationships, to contemplate the simple fact that relationship is only possible on the basis of a comprehensive unity expressed in relationship, and that unity is a universal at once upholding and vanquishing the antagonism of subject and object.

Hieratic doctrines of this kind might seem irritatingly out of place in the sphere of musicology, especially when musicology commits itself to uphold the methods of science at the expense of metaphysical categories whose truth or otherwise musicologists feel to be irrelevant to the matter in hand. However, with specific reference to music, it must be insisted that the analysis of human experience can only be grounded in synthesis. Before we can significantly analyse a musical experience, or that which occasions it, we already imply the unity of what we analyse. Analysis draws out relationships; but these are first established by unified perception, or assumed under a unifying concept. This is a truth that imitators of scientific method, unlike scientists themselves, do not always appreciate. The basic faith of the advanced scientific mind is the unity of the natural order, and it determines the nature of scientific analysis. Too often in musicology, we forget – or ignore – this scientific faith, and commence our analytical operations upon music without any sense of significant order or direction.

It is a highly thought-provoking fact that the rise and establishment of the sonata-principle corresponded in the most intimate way with the gradual emergence and full flowering of a comprehensive metaphysical system which, in so many respects, is the ultimate rationale of the logic of the sonata-principle. Ideally, one has a wordless insight into this profound and subtle matter; in words one can do little more than employ the language of analogy. The Hegelian system, at its finest, is a superb justification of the sonata-principle. Similarly, the classical sonata, at its finest, is a sensuous embodiment of the dialectical relationship of opposed terms. In the collective consciousness of late eighteenth-century man, some vital force was at work which found expression in music, literature and philosophy – in Haydn, Mozart and Beethoven, in Goethe, in Hegel. It was the same force. It found diverse expressions. If we have ears to hear, and minds to understand, how can we refuse this marriage of imagination and reason? How can we persist, as so often we do, in ignoring the tree even as we desire its fruits? Is it not better to strive for a comprehensive, synthetic understanding which at once unlocks the innermost secrets of music and philosophy, and in doing this reveals the innermost nature of the mind . . .?

When, therefore, we approach the sonatas of Emanuel Bach, we are considering manifestations of the creative consciousness which were intimately bound up with a wave of mental and spiritual activity which rippled through the entire field of art and philosophy. This wave aimed directly at a new honesty and a new synthesis – honesty in forwarding the claims of human feeling and emotion, synthesis of the varied and conflicting terms in which feeling and emotion must necessarily be expressed. In Bach's music, a new truth is being propounded, a psychological insight is being erected into a consistent musical attitude and the result is the consolidation of the sonata-principle.

The spirit of the opening movement of the first sonata in the 'Württemberg' set is not unlike the rondo entitled 'Farewell to my Clavichord'. The movement is not a very inspiring one. It employs figurative devices standard to Emanuel's style:

EX. 61

After the first dramatic opening, a contrasting passage follows with romantic overtones. This serves as a bridge leading to the key of E minor (dominant), when the opening theme is restated in the bass against a slender counter-subject. Then follows a modulating and sequential secondary theme. There are two statements of this, divided by a touching twofold 'query':

EX. 62

Development centres mainly upon the bridge material and adds considerably to the length of the movement. The query-phrase just quoted also comes in for more extended treatment:

EX. 63

and the opening theme, when it is finally recapitulated, is further developed. The movement is not monothematic; but the prevalence of the arpeggio (marked *) in EX. 61 creates the illusion that it is, as also does the repetition of the opening theme when the bridge has already established the dominant key.

The lovely slow movement is full of melting figures, and it is characterized by a rising theme which one associates frequently with Mozart:

EX. 64

Especially beautiful is the languishing and wistful rhapsody which comes near the end of this little song. It is an early anticipation of the pianoforte soliloquy which concludes Schumann's *Dichterliebe*. This impression is heightened if one avails onself of the opportunity for a cadenza which the cadential 6/4 allows. It was the custom not only in concertos, but also in keyboard sonatas, to write these 6/4 chords near the end of a composition

and to inscribe a pause-mark over them. The performer was then free
to improvise upon the thematic material of the piece. Clementi is very
fond of the device. It is worth quoting the relevant passage from Bach's
sonata in full:

EX. 65

The finale begins with a theme which is structurally related to the
theme of the slow movement and also characterized by a falling figure
from the first:

EX. 66

In conception and execution it is extremely successful, being full of the
liveliest tunes and spiced with unexpected sounds which demand a sense
of bravura at the keyboard:

EX. 67

The second sonata begins far more sweetly than the first and soon leads
off into a rippling figure anticipating the *chiaroscuro* of Hummel:

EX. 68

This semiquaver pattern is related to the opening material as an
extension to its primary generating statement, and it becomes highly
important to the overall form of the movement. In fact, it becomes a
binding thread.

The other thematic material consists of fairly short phrases ending with
a pause and they are coloured strongly by emotional sighs and expressive
appogiaturas. Throughout the entire movement, great use is made of
adagio phrase-endings, and recommencements in a brisk manner which
in turn are overcome by an affecting sigh and contrasting dynamics.

The middle movement further develops the interplay of contrasting
piano and forte and gives a more considered treatment of moments
already anticipated in the previous movements:

EXX. 69a, b

Apart from phrases of this type, the rest of the movement is remarkable
for its lyrical, concerto-like freedom – indeed, the whole sonata lives in a

far more expansive sphere than most of his earlier work, and one senses the increasing confidence of the composer and the readier flow of inspiration:

EX. 70

This last observation is especially true of the finale which shows a sense of keyboard 'spread' far more liberal than that of the 'Prussian' set. There is the same preponderance of expressive appogiaturas as in the other two movements:

EX. 71

and a fondness for arpeggiation in the accompanimental figuration:

EX. 72

The third sonata contains a remarkable mass of conflicting material, and one senses the presence of something almost grotesque at work in the mental processes of a composer who yet committed himself so whole-heartedly to melodic types which later became accepted features of the conventional classical manner. The first movement of this sonata will be worth an extended analysis.

The opening gesture is tremendous – a veritable challenge in the grand manner, abounding in crushed notes, and as powerful an opening for a sonata as the most grandiose formal scheme could require:

EX. 73

But if this passage were to be offered to students in an examination together with the invitation to sketch a suitable follow-on, how many would hit upon anything remotely akin to what Bach then wrote?

EX. 74

Paradoxically, this seemingly fatuous passage betrays Bach's reputable musical origins. The psychological impact of the opening passage is here reorientated in the light of a new formal ideal; but it has affinities with the toccata-style of Buxtehude, who was addicted to repeated notes in toccatas and fugues and other pieces.

EX. 75

Canzonetta   *D. Buxtehude*

Equally breath-taking is the way the toccata-motif is suavely dismissed by a phrase of the purest and most conventional classicism:

EX. 76

This serves to introduce a theme with which we are already familiar (EX. 48) and this, with sublime affected innocence, is then accompanied by EX. 74. We have here a case exactly analogous to the build-up in the finale of Beethoven's 'Eroica' Symphony, when a bass-motif is heard before the theme to which it is later going to serve as an accompaniment. In due course, the scrap of conventional classicism moves into the left-hand part, and the toccata-figure takes on a more assertive status in the right:

EX. 77

There is a momentary return to the latter part of the opening figure:

EX. 78

and then the exposition quickly ends with a last echo of the toccata. Throughout the development and recapitulation which, as in the fourth 'Prussian' sonata, are somewhat closely integrated, Bach devotes himself to the synthesis of conflicting material he has laid out in the exposition. He achieves this with considerable success, primarily by means of a powerful and dissonant extension of the opening theme – which, it is now obvious, is a dramatic recitative – by extension of the toccata-passage, and sequential treatment of the classical theme. This amounts to a developmental restatement of all the main ideas in a more extreme and pungent form. It is worth observing at this point that antitheses in subjective experience are generally more extreme and tense before they are finally transcended. In some sense, these very forces of repulsion and conflict which are at work in the development of the primary tensions seem to generate their opposite, the forces of attraction which bring about the eventual fusion of the thematic elements. Anyone who really observes his own psychological tensions knows this to be true – bearing in mind that the tensions and conflicts one simply forgets were never real anti-theses, and that merely forgetting or losing the sense of impact of an experience is not, in any sense, the meaning of transcendence. The sonata-principle, in the functions of its middle phase, generally drives a wedge into conflicts already exposed, and heightens the sense of anti-thesis to a maximum in order to bring about a sense of crisis.

At any rate, after giving the primary material a substantial develop-mental 'roughing-up', Bach has still not finished with the toccata-motif, the initial dissonances of which are now intensified and then associated with a wistful phrase recollecting the second subject:

EX. 79

This takes us straight back to the opening recitative which, in turn, introduces the recapitulated second subject without the further individualistic intrusion of EX. 74. Before the movement ends, the second subject is heightened by a 'farewell' phrase:

EX. 80

The toccata-figure has the last word.

The slow movement is a model of beauty and grace in a very similar style to the adagio of the previous sonata. Particularly interesting is the extension of an originally continuous figure from the opening theme by a threefold augmentation and expressive rests:

EXX. 81a, b

and there are echoes of EX. 80.

The fourth sonata is very baroque in spirit. It opens in a mid-eighteenth-century manner but reverts quickly to an earlier style. At times we seem to be listening to a concerted work in the Handelian manner:

EX. 82

The slow movement looks and sounds like a three-part invention, which is really what it is:

EX. 83

The baroque feeling is also present in a Vivaldi-like figure in the finale:

EX. 84

which, however, when taken as a whole, has more of an early Haydn quality. Compare the opening theme, and its subsequent career, with the finale of a Sonata in G by Haydn:

EXX. 85a, b

The fifth sonata is virtually monothematic in its first movement, and it seems to be an experimental type of composition in this respect. Bach is less interested in thematic contrast here than in the exploitation of rhythmic figures. These often have a complex structure and, as in the previous work, a baroque flavour. Dotted-note patterns abound. Here are two characteristic passages:

EXX. 86a, b

It is the rhythmic variety of this first movement which stamps it as forward-looking and modern in relation to the more conventional utterances of many of Emanuel's contemporaries. And this is the place to repeat that the conflict and stress of the sonata-idiom is not, of course, merely a matter of thematic contrast. Frequently it is more a matter of key-contrast and rhythmic fragmentation. Largely because of Beethoven, whose contrasts nevertheless are at once rhythmic, thematic and tonal, we tend to look instinctively for conflicting themes. When Emanuel Bach concentrates his creative impulse into the sphere of rhythm and key-relationships, the result, as here, is frequently one of dynamic abstraction. The movement under discussion has a very 'solid' intellectual appeal.

The polyphony of the adagio is again a backward glance to the free counterpoint in the preludes of J. S. Bach. Its opening theme should be compared with that of the finale:

EXX. 87a, b

The finale again reveals what Haydn learned from Emanuel Bach, especially in respect of the significant use of repeated notes in thematic material:

EX. 88a

The finale of a famous sonata by Haydn is reminiscent of this:

EX. 88b

The last of the 'Württemberg' set is a fascinating composition, highly experimental in tone, not at all gracious to the hands, and severely intellectual throughout. Its refusal to consort with mere tunefulness, its ruthless rhythmic drive, and the vigorous counterpoint in the finale make it a fitting companionpiece to a powerful sonata in the same key by Clementi.[3]

In this work a number of traditional features are brought to a focus by and in the sonata-principle. The first movement is monothematic, and it combines dramatic recitative with the spirit of the French Overture. In the general extension of ideas and in the development proper, the first movement exhibits the spirit of a fantasia. The slow movement has a fine classical theme – a veritable romantic lament; but this rapidly succumbs to the rhythmic pressure which pervades the entire sonata. Here it is manifested in repeated and dotted-note patterns:

EX. 89

It is in the finale that comparison with Clementi's B minor sonata becomes irresistible. Here all is severely logical. A remorseless drive permeates a satisfyingly long movement, and establishes a fitting conclusion to the work:

EX. 90

Chapter nine

C. P. E. Bach and the Sonata (*4*)
The Probe-Stücke

THESE compositions appeared together with the 1753 edition of the *Versuch*, and serve to give point to the practical instruction contained in that work. The first three sonatas seem designed to give the student practice in mastering those fingering problems arising mainly from elaborate ornamentation. Their musical content is generally unremarkable and does not advance the compositional standpoint reached in the 'Württemberg' set.

The first sonata is built up of three song-like movements, the keys of which express the notes of the triad of C major. The first movement is in C, the second in E minor, the third in G major. By a similar device, the keys of the movements in the second sonata express the G minor triad in descending order, the first movement being in D minor, the second in B flat, the third in G minor. Beethoven employs a similar arrangement in the late Bagatelles. In the third sonata, the three movements are contained by the open fifth – I, A major – II, A minor – III, E major.

For the most part, two-voice textures prevail, with occasional chords for colouring and harmonic strength. Dance-forms are employed. The first sonata ends with a minuetto, the second with a jig; whereas the first movement of the third is very similar to the kind of minuet Haydn used to compose in his pianoforte sonatas:

EXX. 91a, b

The idiom is occasionally kittenish in the quick movements and senti-
mental in the slower ones. The most satisfyingly worked-out scheme is in
the finale of the third sonata, which is a sonata-allegro embodying no
thematic contrasts. A poetic melody pursues a gentle meandering course
through a chain of conventional modulations. Its vicissitudes are purely
melodic, and frequently lead to some beautiful figuration. The texture is
in two parts throughout:

EX. 92

This music has the delicacy and intricate poetry of Mozart.

The last three sonatas are in a different category, and are amongst
C. P. E. Bach's finest compositions for the keyboard. If the first three are
primarily for the performer of modest attainments, the second group
require more mature insight and accomplishment. Numbers four and six
especially are characterized by a profound nobility of utterance.

The keys of the movements of the fourth sonata express the notes of
the triad of B minor; those of the fifth sonata are a fifth apart (is Bach
indulging in a play upon numbers here?), whereas the key-relationships
of the sixth are defined by the triad of F minor – taking the last movement as the 'Hamlet' Fantasia in C minor, which completes the key-
scheme of the whole set of six.

The fourth sonata is a magnificent composition, very solidly constructed, and given an underlying unity of conception by the basic
triadic relationship of the movements and the thematic unity of the
opening figures of the first and last movements:

EXX. 93a, b

The slow movement is composed in a blend of archaic dotted-note rhythms, modern (by eighteenth-century standards) harmonies and a melodic keyboard recitative of a style peculiar to C. P. E. Bach. The virtue of this particular movement is that here elements are fused by an intense concentration of texture which never for a second releases its subjective pressure. The following quotation is a fair example of the style of the movement. The climactic moment here is harmonic rather than dynamic (X). In the subsequent arpeggiation, the bass-note shifts before the point of resolution:

EX. 94

Towards the end, Bach dispenses with bar-lines, and plunges into free fantasia, with an extensive use of keyboard vibrato:

EX. 95

The finale is in binary form with two main themes, the first of which has already been quoted. The preponderance of other thematic fragments in this charming Siciliano gives it a rondo atmosphere. Most noteworthy is the treatment of the chords at the end of the descending scale of the first subject in its recapitulation:

EX. 96

There is something curiously modern about this entire movement. Indeed, the strange combination of detailed figuration, intense harmony and sometimes tenuous counterpoint pervading the whole sonata, anticipates a manner of which Hindemith is very fond. The following is both unusual and appealing by any standards:

EX. 97

Compare this fragment from *Ludus Tonalis*:

EX. 98

The first movement of the fifth sonata is not very interesting – a finger exercise without more than technical content.

The adagio, however, is a most beautiful work, an aria for keyboard, music which invokes those very emotions it expresses, and by any standards a lovely piece of musical craftsmanship. It is in a movement of this type that we touch the nerve of Emanuel Bach's aesthetic, and contemplate a realized aspect of his musical ideal. Every note in every ornament contributes its expressive burden to the whole. It is possible to write out the notational implications of a passage like this:

EX. 99

but how can notes remotely convey the rhythmic subtlety, the minute rubato of the turns, the rendering of the metrical pulse in the bass? Performance on a modern pianoforte can give no inkling of the real music buried in this notation. A sensitive clavichord is necessary – ideally, one could wish to hear a Silbermann instrument played by the master himself! We should remember that the performance of repeated chords in a simple accompaniment is precisely where so many performers *pro antiqua* reveal a gross lack of sensitivity. Are they to be mere mechanical thumps marking the metrical beat? Or are they to be tonal pulsations echoing the throb of the human heart, the passions of which are felt down to the end of the clavichordist's finger-tips?

EX. 100

The plangent passage concluding the movement is a further demonstration of his expressive purpose:

EX. 101

The finale is a delicate Mozartean rondo, the final statement of the main theme being varied. This piece strikes a fantastically inconsequential note after the adagio, and its intricate phrasing, whilst no doubt providing exercise for the fingers, is not especially pleasing to listeners attuned to the superior grace of Haydn or Mozart. It is one of those works where justification may be found in what was then Bach's didactic purpose.

If the final fantasia is to be considered integrally with the allegro in F minor and the adagio in A flat, then we must acknowledge that the three movements, considered as clavichord and not as piano music, constitute a noble and impressive composition. A remarkable fact must be noted about the work thus considered. Apart from the relatively short E flat major section of the fantasia, all the melodic writing in the sonata is compressed into the adagio; the rest of the fantasia is recitative, and the whole of the first movement is highly coloured impressionistic figuration, the real force of which comes more from its rhythmic impetus than from any thematic content. Such thematic material as emerges from time to time is short and fragmentary; but in virtue of the rhythmic impulse it carries tremendous impact:

EX. 102

This is the kind of writing which is found throughout Beethoven's entire keyboard output, and most frequently in his earlier compositions. The *Sonate Pathétique* springs readily to mind, and indeed this sonata of Bach's anticipates the technique of the first movement of that work.

Another delightful feature of this movement is the harmonic reversal of EX. 102 in recapitulation. Instead of A flat to F minor, we now find B flat minor to G flat major:

EX. 103

This is a master-stroke of tonal imagination in a pungent movement which ends only a few bars later in the key of F minor.

The adagio is a prolonged cantilena, with scarcely a rest in the melodic part from beginning to end of the piece. Haydn, observed Shedlock,[1] was Bach's pupil, but Beethoven was his spiritual heir. So much is now obvious to us. It is possible to over-emphasize Bach's anticipations of later composers: but perhaps we can be forgiven for glimpsing something of the harmonic richness of Schubert also in this switch from major to minor:

EX. 104

Even Brahms was attached to the arpeggiation-device which Bach here employs in the accompaniment. The movement ends with a bar-less rhapsody, like the adagio in the fourth sonata.

Chapter ten

C. P. E. Bach and the Sonata (5)
The 'Sonatas with Altered Reprises'

Des qu'on se répète aujourd'hui, et qu'on reproduit une chose, il est indispensable d'y faire des changemens.

Preface to the *Sonaten mit veränderten Reprisen*

EMANUEL Bach's *Sonaten mit veränderten Reprisen* ('Sonatas with Altered Reprises') were composed largely to give musical substance to his belief that ornamentation is an essential part of musical performance. This is quite clearly brought out in the lengthy Preface to the 1760 edition, where he writes:

'Dans la composition de ces Sonates, j'ai principalement en vue ces Commençans et ces Amateurs, qui, à cause du nombre de leurs années, ou de leur occupations, n'ont, ni le tems, ni la patience de se livrer à des exercices d'une certaine difficulté. J'ai voulu leur procurer les moyens aisés de se procurer et aux autres la satisfaction d'accompagner de quelque changemens les Pieces qu'ils executent, sans qu'ils ayent besoin pour cela de les inventer eux-mêmes, ou de recouvrir à d'autres qui leur prescrivent des choses qu'ils n'apprendoient qu'avec une extreme peine.'

On the surface, Bach always seems to have in mind the applause of the listener for a finely embellished cadence or a skilfully embroidered melody, and even for a cadenza executed with verve and dash. Upon a closer examination, his own music, together with his remarks about it, indicate clearly enough that performer and composer are to be considered a closely integrated pair. Ornamentation is itself a vital aspect of musical thought – a spontaneous outflow of sensibility which must be immediately disciplined by the formal structure. The didactic function of these sonatas was to drive home Emanuel's passionately held conviction that ornamentation is not something which may be arbitrarily imposed upon the thematic content of a piece during an inconsequential performance. By insisting upon this point, Bach not only subscribed to the need for a pleasing variety, but also paved the way for a more organic conception of sonata-form. Organically conceived sonata-form movements continue their growth right up to the final chord. Stereotyped movements tend to recapitulate previously exposed material with the minimal alteration of the reprise required to conclude the music in the tonic key. Schubert's restatements, for example, are sometimes little more than transposed expositions – where the piano sonatas are concerned. In the symphonies and chamber music of Haydn and Mozart there are, on the other hand, many subtle modifications of basic thematic material in the recapitulations. There is a particularly lovely alteration in the reprise of the second subject of the first movement of Mozart's thirty-ninth symphony. Variety of restatement is really a *sine qua non* of the sonata-principle.

The finer musical minds of the eighteenth century knew full well that the art of ornamentation involved much more than the addition of external decorations to a plain tune. In the best melodies of François Couperin, virtually nothing is left if the ornaments are removed, so beautifully are they integrated by the overall expressive impulse. Bach's convictions about this matter evidently went very deep, and it is interesting to consider his inner aesthetic motivation in the light of published copies of the 'Sonatas with Altered Reprises' which have found their way into the libraries at Paris and Brussels, and also in the British Museum. These copies passed through Emanuel's hands, and on each one he has inscribed marginal alterations to the printed text which throw much light on the subject under discussion. In some cases, the original alterations to the reprise are elaborated; in others, the initial thematic material is itself elaborated. A general review of these afterthoughts invites the conclusion that the revisions are all in favour of a more subtle interpretation and a more advanced clavier technique than Bach had in mind when he first composed the sonatas. The total effect of the revisions is one of liberation from the somewhat tightly knit and often rather stiff and formalistic patterns of the original compositions. They are very much in the spirit of the running passages in the fantasia *C. P. E. Bachs Empfindungen* and the famous *Abschied*, and they show how far Bach moved in his later years towards a fluent and pliable romantic lyricism.

In some cases, a simple quadruple grouping of semiquavers is turned into a triplet pattern. In every case the marginal additions are concerned with melody and more notes are required than in the original version. The most forward-looking changes anticipate Hummel's practice of packing large groups of fast notes into single bars moving in slow tempo, and it is the fifth sonata of the set on which the composer has lavished the most careful retrospective thought. The overall form remains unchanged but the melodic outline has modifications in each movement. This sonata (which, incidentally, may be seen in its unaltered form in Peters Edition No. 4188) is in three long movements. The first two, 'poco allegro' and 'larghetto' are dominated by that detailed exploitation of sentiment which is such a feature of Bach's ruminating style; but in the original version the melodic line often has a stilted and manufactured sound. His emotions may have been genuine enough, but the expressive impulse probably lingered too long in the brain before it reached the keyboard. However, the alterations in the fifth sonata suggests that the composer was aware of this. In every case, revision has resulted in an emancipation of the melodic outline from its earlier stiff and stilted manner. One feels that a more rubato style of performance occupied Bach in his later years. One example will suffice to indicate this more fluid manner, and it is taken from the finale, a rondo-minuet. The opening theme has affinities with that of the first movement, and both movements make much use of a rising arpeggio in B flat. In its original form, this appears on page 28 of the 1760 edition as:

EX. 105

but Bach altered it to:

EX. 106

In the library of the Paris Conservatoire, the copy which evidently passed through Emanuel's hands contains this amendment in red ink. Most importantly, the date 1788 is inscribed at the foot of the last page of the sonata – also in red ink, and undoubtedly by the same hand which altered the musical notation. Emanuel died in 1788. The Paris copy contains no other alterations.

The implications seem to be that Bach made the more comprehensive revisions in the copy now in the British Museum after the single altera-tion in the Paris version. Perhaps this last touched off the desire to work thoroughly over the rest of the fifth sonata, and subsequently through the entire set. If the date is a true indication of the time when the revisions were carried out, then it is possible that these afterthoughts were also among his last thoughts.

A close comparison of Bach's modifications with the keyboard style of later composers like Dusík and Hummel who embraced the fluid, romantic style which we instinctively associate with Chopin, its finest exponent, reveals the tremendous strides made by Emanuel in the development of keyboard technique. C. P. E. Bach's musical consciousness spanned the eighteenth century, building a bridge between baroque procedures and the earlier phases of classicism. The composer of church cantatas was able to anticipate the piano style developed after his death. The man who could construct masterly keyboard fugues was able to explore a refined, lyrical technique of musical expression.

It is highly significant that Bach, in his *Autobiography*, refers to his efforts to acquire a singing manner of keyboard performance:

> 'My chief study, particularly in later years, has been directed towards playing the *clavier* (despite its deficiency in sustaining power), so that playing should be as much like singing as possible. This task is not very easy, if the ear is not to be starved, nor the noble simplicity of the song spoiled by overmuch noise.
>
> As I see it, music should move the heart emotionally, and a player will never achieve this by mere scrambling, hammering and arpeggiation, not with me anyway.'

The word *clavier* has been left untranslated in the above passage. Obviously it refers either to the clavichord, pianoforte or both – but almost certainly not to the harpsichord. During his long sojourn at the Prussian Court, Emanuel would have had ample opportunity of exploring the possibilities of the many Silbermann pianos purchased by King Frederick. Later on, at Hamburg, he was able to investigate the very newest instruments, and almost certainly he was able to envisage the future of the piano as a singing instrument. It should certainly not be forgotten, however, that Emanuel Bach loved Gottfried Silbermann's clavichords which had a greater sonority and sensitivity than the unsophisticated instruments of earlier days, and that one of his most moving, song-like compositions, the famous *Abschied vom Silbermannschen Clavier*, was written for the clavichord.

It is highly likely that because of this concentration upon lyrical performance Bach was able to develop a keyboard style which strongly influenced that of J. L. Dusík who took lessons from him in Berlin, and who visited him at Hamburg in 1783. A glance at Dusík's keyboard sonatas will reveal at once that his techniques of thematic elaboration and variation closely resemble those of C. P. E. Bach, and there are some running passages exactly like those written into the Sonatas with Altered Reprises. If Dusík, like Burney, was regaled by Emanuel with hours of inspired improvisation, one feels that it must have made a deep impression upon him. It is also interesting to speculate upon the content of their conversation. Did Dusík, whose inner ear seemed to be attuned to the flow of distant waters, extol the virtues of the new pianofortes over those of the clavichord? Did Bach, in his turn, aver the supremacy of the traditional instrument? The fact that they met is in itself important for the history of pianoforte music, and it goes some way to support the notion of a continuously unfolding keyboard tradition from C. P. E. Bach to Chopin. In this tradition, the Sonatas with Altered Reprises, and not least the amendments which Emanuel made in the last year of his life, play a not unimportant part.

Chapter eleven

C. P. E. Bach and the Sonata (6)
The 'Sonatas for Connoisseurs and Amateurs'

THE sonatas in the great collections *für Kenner und Liebhaber* ('Sonatas for Connoisseurs and Amateurs') contain a vast amount of unusual and varied music. There are movements when the level of inspiration is not notably high; but remembering the point made at the beginning of this book about the polarities of sound and intellect, it is at least hospitable to try and grasp the innermost intention when the sound – especially on a modern pianoforte – is not as exciting as we could wish. There is a further point of some importance. Composers are not always writing consciously for posterity, and there is room for the manufacture of pleasant expendable music in the idiom of the day which does not embody a sense of spiritual striving or aim at large concert audiences. Hindemith's conception of utility-music is not entirely out of place. Whether his attempted justifications are rejected or not, it remains true that much music is being composed at the present time which is neither pleasant, useful in any sense whatever, nor likely to endure.

With regard to the tonal effect of these compositions, it must be stressed, once again, that pianoforte performance detracts from their beauty. We play J. S. Bach on a piano and, on the whole, enjoy the result. On a good clavichord we should enjoy much of it more. It is true that Bach published the collections for Connoisseurs and Amateurs with the fortepiano in mind, and some of his compositions have appeared recently in fortepiano recordings. However, it remains true that Bach approached the fortepiano in terms of a keyboard style far more appropriate to the clavichord than to the newer instrument. He retains the unconscious presuppositions of a clavichord composer *par excellence*. In any case, the medium of a modern pianoforte is largely an anachronism in the case of Emanuel Bach. There is far less room for compromise, since the nature of his musical thinking is far more closely integrated with the technique of the clavichord than that of his father, and with a mode of addressing the clavichord which, in Emanuel's mind, amounted to an individualistic philosophy of performance. What kind of sense could the most sensitive pianist make of the following passage on a modern Steinway?

EX. 107

In these later sonatas we find a compendium of all Bach's musical devices, an encyclopaedic collection of all the elements that he finally fused in his personal style. A sonata, for C. P. E. Bach, is a little world – a subjective world. This world is made up of emotional effects between which there is an element of conflict and tension. This conflict is expressed between the contrasting movements of which a sonata is composed, and more vitally in the swift succession of passages differentiated in terms of thematic structure, rhythm and harmonic relationship which occurs particularly in movements of the sonata-form type. The outward dialectical discipline which is the direct musical result of the new emotional honesty of the Berlin school of aesthetic, to which Bach wholeheartedly subscribed, is finally fused, in the last sonatas, with the sonata-form concept, the result being a vigorous and challenging affirmation of the sonata-principle, the mode of musical thought which reflects the most penetrating metaphysical insight of the day. Wholeness is movement. Movement is tension. Tension is subjective. Subjectivity negates itself in objectivity. Objectivity establishes itself in form. Form expresses wholeness. Being is Becoming, and transcends the opposition of subject and object.

Let it be stressed that Bach was no mere speculator, and I would be the last to maintain that Bach's sonatas were *consciously* influenced by any metaphysical ideal. That is not my point. In any case, the period of Bach's intellectual development as composer and theorist was prior to the Schelling-Hegel-Goethe phase, the real musical correlative of which is the music of Beethoven.[1] In the sphere of philosophy, however, Lessing and the *Sturm und Drang* school had really defined the basic tensions of the subjective consciousness which Hegel and Goethe, in their respective ways, had to acknowledge. Their problem was one of reconciliation with the objective order; before they could solve it, they had to accept the inner dialectic of the soul (the modern psychologist would think in terms of conflicting elements emerging from the unconscious) and then seek a universal category of philosophical understanding (Hegel) or poetic insight (Goethe) which would show the fundamental unity of the inner and outer worlds.

One does not have to be a philosopher to become sensitive to a meta-physical trend – to a current of life-force which can find all manner of diverse expressions. As we have seen, the poets Lessing and Klopstock were frequent guests at Emanuel's house in Hamburg, as were many of the intelligentsia. They must frequently have discussed the aesthetic of expressionism, and their discussions must have added fuel to the inner ferment of their creative consciousness. What seems so obvious at this distance of time is the growth and impact of a universal trend of thought, a trend associated, ultimately, with spiritual aspiration once the varied impulsions of subjective life had been metaphysically bound to a philoso-phical ideal of unity.

In Emanuel Bach's mind, we can be certain that the formal integration of a subjective content was not bound by a *philosophical* ideal; but this, as I see it, is only to acknowledge that ideals are often, in their most potent implications, far more profound than we imagine them to be. In laying hold of a certain principle, we do not always realize that we are furthering a new mode of life-expression. In planting the sapling we seldom visualize the tree which will afford shade for our descendants. But the same life-force expresses itself in both.

The sonatas of Bach's later years are bound to those of Beethoven by a spiritual principle which it is virtually certain neither composer reflected upon. The word 'spiritual' is here divested of its orthodox associations, and used in a minimal sense to denote the intangible, invisible informing positive polarity of the creative human consciousness, that to which the sphere of musical tone is feminine or negative. There need be no religious overtones at all. It is enough to grant that in the sphere of musical history and criticism there are occasions when it is insufficient to ignore the indwelling causes of tonal effects. The last sonatas of Emanuel Bach are a challenge to our critical faculties, and our historical insight into the growth of the musical mind.

Book I

In the first volume (1779) sonatas 2, 4 and 6 are of considerable substance; the other three all have at least one movement containing interesting features.

The first sonata in C begins with a solfeggio to be played prestissimo, and really looks backward to the preamble or study-type of composition popular in earlier times. In the midst of all these scampering semiquavers which, on a clavichord, give a feverish buzz, the odd bar in crotchets (EX. 107) which introduces the recapitulation strikes a very curious note.

The second sonata in F major is an altogether more elaborate composition. The thematic structure of the first movement is highly complex from a rhythmic point of view, and is further complicated by the employment of a considerable variety of ornaments. This example is a fair sample of its intricate style – which cannot easily be fathomed by a modern performer unless he is prepared to take great pains with it and exercise his historical imagination to the utmost.

EX. 108

A further passage taken from the development, which combines dissonance with vibrato, has quite a modern appearance. In fact, there is nothing quite like it in the music of any other composer – though we might be tempted to listen more attentively to the electrifying extension of 'Muss es sein?' which occurs in the development of the finale of Beethoven's opus 135:

EX. 109

On a modern pianoforte, this vibrato is certainly not obtainable. Something akin to a *Bebung* can be produced with an extremely relaxed wrist. The dampers must be lifted, and the performer should strive for rapid repetitions combined with sudden crescendo over each chord. A subterfuge of this kind will at any rate enable the performer to savour something of the strangeness of this highly imaginative writing, even if it is impossible to play a true vibrato.

This remarkable movement ends with a transition to the Larghetto which follows at once in the key of F minor. For all its economy of means this transition is remarkably impressive:

EX. 110

Without doubt the Larghetto is one of Bach's finest creations. There are moments which echo the strange sounds of EX. 109:

EX. 111

and the entire movement abounds in the most moving poetic utterances, in which it is no exaggeration to say that Bach captures moments of real inspiration:

EX. 112

In this example, the bass is to be played as melodically and as impressively as possible. It is part of the song.

After two intense movements, a finale in lighter vein is to be expected; but the performer can be excused if he finds it thematically unsatisfying. Nevertheless, it is conceived and executed with a sure touch.

Sonata 3 consists of allegretto and finale in B minor and a slow movement in G minor. There is a suggestion of thematic unity about the three movements:

EXX. 113a, b, c

The first movement is monothematic, the andante, apart from its opening phrase, is largely non-thematic, and consists almost entirely of rhythmic figuration worked out against an adventurous modulatory scheme – which, of course, moves towards the key of the finale. The finale itself, marked cantabile, is a kind of passacaglia – the theme undergoing successive variation over an austerely repetitive bass:

EX. 114

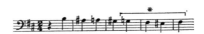

Davison and Apel offer it as an example of Bach's affecting style in their *Historical Anthology*.

It is of some interest to compare the bass just quoted with the descending bass notes at the end of the previous movements:

EX. 115

Figure * is also foreshadowed in the first line of the opening movement:

EX. 116

How far conscious intellectualism was at work in this sonata it is interesting to consider.

The sonata in A which follows has a first movement characterized by a very orthodox classical sound. It is a fully developed movement rather in the manner of Johann Christian Bach, and is basically monothematic. Emanuel employs an accompanimental figure popular with both Haydn and Clementi. It is an obvious way of giving a little snap and zest to a series of repeated notes:

EX. 117a

EX. 117b, c

The allegro does not reach a final close in the tonic, but leads to a few preparatory bars in F sharp minor.

The orthodox classical geometry of the allegro does not remotely prepare us for the ethereal beauty of the 'poco adagio' which now engages the ear. It is as delicate as a nocturne by Chopin, and in its fine attention to details of formal construction anticipates Hindemith's style in slow arioso melodies.

EX. 118

The first movement is rigidly dated by its opening bars. The second would add grace and poetry to any modern concert-programme. In this case, the curling figuration does not lose its freshness on the pianoforte keyboard. It is, moreover, a fine study in sensitive and delicate playing.

In the finale we have a movement which has found its way into many piano albums. In spirit and key it is not unlike the finale of a popular sonata by Mozart in D major, and it reverts to the neat classicism of the first movement.

This may be the best place to observe that Bach's later style contains many anticipations of the standard classical manner as it is expressed, for example, in the keyboard sonatas of Clementi, Mozart and Haydn. But between the survivals of the baroque spirit, the essays in rococo and *stile galante*, the rounded classical movements, there is something unique and personal to Emanuel Bach. In general, we would prefer this unique and personal quality to those characteristics which are more obviously in line with the orthodox Viennese tradition. The present sonata is more to be prized, perhaps, for its adagio, than for the undoubtedly well-executed Viennese-type movements in which it is framed. We might well consider that this sonata is altogether more successful as a work of art than the second or third already discussed. And yet, in the last analysis, is it as interesting or provocative?

In the fifth sonata Bach reverts to this provocative manner. It begins like the opening of an introspective string-quartet; the wedge-shaped progression of the first three chords in each bar seems deliberately designed to emphasize the augmented chord. The sonata also begins in the 'wrong' key:

EX. 119

The trite follow-on, however, is disappointing. The inchoate striving makes a temporary break-through; but there is insufficient thrust to sustain the impact of this highly imaginative gesture. Bach looks feebly to conventional patterns.

This is followed by a solemn 'adagio maestoso', full of interesting things despite its brevity. The reprise is introduced by a phrase related to EX. 119:

EX. 120

and the tonal palette is enhanced by a few bars of wider harmonic spacing which contrast expressively with the closely worked harmony of the main theme. The finale begins in the 'wrong' key; but otherwise proceeds in a conventional manner.

Sonata no. 6 in G is a *tour de force* in Bach's grand virtuoso style. Thematic interest is entirely subordinated in the first movement to the conflict between dynamic scraps of rhythmic figuration. The texture is highly dichotomized – one might almost say 'atomistic' – and cannot be adequately illustrated by a quotation since the atomic elements are so different from one another. This sort of movement reveals the emptiness of the textbook attitude to sonata-form, yet shows what Bach really contributed to the rise of the sonata-principle. Disdaining reliance upon traditional contrapuntal textures, which he well knew how to compose, and which would have lightened his compositional tasks, he confronted the mass of conflicting raw material which erupted in his mind, and sought persistently for the principle of unity. Unlike Mozart, he didn't 'hear it all at once' – that kind of insight into the multiplicity of tonal elements had not yet arrived on the musical scene. He simply had to think out the formal problems involved. In some cases he hit upon a strikingly successful solution. In this movement, he grasps the formal value of dramatic preparation of the reprise. The opening theme, following a precedent in the exposition, is roughly treated, and then exploded in a cascade of notes leading straight back to its formal restatement:

EXX. 121a, b

The andante is a very loose and rhapsodic binary structure. Its texture has a skeletal aspect owing to the preponderance of thin two-part writing – one part of which is often no more than a few isolated crotchets or minims, the other being a wayward trickle of improvisatory figuration. The movement is, in fact, an improvisation, and the same style is perpetuated in the finale which is to be played very fast. Hence the rhapsodic structure results in a heterogeneous fantasia of keyboard effects characterized by features which a modern pianist, confronting these pages for the first time, must surely find very odd. Ultra-rapid arpeggiation stops abruptly, isolated chords hang bewilderingly in space, progressions of arpeggios lead to affecting little cadences, the harmony being seldom more than a two-part structure which even Grétry (between whose parts, it was once said, one could drive a coach and four) did not outstretch. I quote an interesting passage without further comment:

EX. 122

Book II

The innocent first sonata, in G, has a very Haydnesque quality.This feature in the exposition of the allegro belies the developmental extremities which follow. It was characteristic of Haydn to submit tuneful material to rigorous extension in the middle section of his sonata-form movements, and it is not impossible that Bach was now under Haydn's influence. There is every musical indication that this was so. Particularly characteristic of Haydn was the transmutation of a theme by use of the mediant minor, a procedure here employed by C. P. E. Bach:

EXX. 123a, b

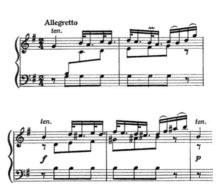

A crudely effective seventh prepares the next movement, which is in the remote key of F sharp minor – another delicate etching full of curling phrases, and touched with the true spirit of rhapsody. The finale is busy and on the whole unexciting, though it has an affecting second subject:

EX. 124

The subsequent treatment of this in the recapitulation reveals the advantage of composing a sectional theme, the different parts of which can be rearranged in a contrasting range of tonalities – to accord, if necessary, with the need for eventual return to a tonic. This, of course, is an established classical principle.

In the second sonata of this set, which is in two movements only, Bach opens with a languishing F major melody which subsequently undergoes variation:

EXX. 125a, b, c, d

The music is a continuous monothematic arioso, all the time unfolding in new twists and turns of decoration, and finally dying away in a progression of dark-toned chords ending in F minor. The joke is that the finale is in a robust F major. There is some affinity with the theme of the first movement (X):

EX. 126

In the third sonata (A major), Bach contrives the effect of a 'sonata quasi una fantasia' in one movement. However, two sections are clearly recognizable, and are linked by a false preparation in the key of C when the finale is clearly A major. The key of A major is nevertheless consistently avoided until the end of the piece, and the first half actually ends in B minor. This kind of device again points to the influence of Haydn. On the other hand, Bach himself had the reputation of being a joker, and it is possible that the influence was reciprocal.

Book III

The first sonata in Volume III is a slight work, the first movement being basically a preludial flourish in A minor shaped by the extended binary outline. The second is a slender two-part effusion, and the third is a jig – introduced and rounded off by an arabesque of rapid notes, like the first movement. A good deal of the writing is exceptionally thin.

The second work in D minor is made of sterner stuff. Ornamented figuration plays a great part throughout the entire composition, but especially in the first movement which strongly embodies the spirit of Domenico Scarlatti:

EX. 127

The 'cantabile e mesto' which follows is a sombre piece in a style often employed by Clementi in his own sonatas. In one passage, Bach's sense of harmonic fitness appears to have yielded to his zest for tonal adventure. The unsatisfactory sound produced by these sevenths may be due to the augmented fourth in the bass:

EX. 128

In the varied reprise, this effect is managed better:

EX. 129

A broken, rather fragmentary manner in the finale gives a dour impression – like one or two of the 'Follia' variations in the same key.

In the third sonata (F minor), we have a well-known piece which breathes the same air as the big A major sonata of Volume I, and also looks forward to the early storm and stress sonatas of Beethoven – especially opus 2, no. 1, which is also in F minor. Particularly noteworthy for purposes of stylistic comparison are the 'Mannheim skyrockets' with which the work opens, and the crudely effective stress chords in the middle of the exposition:

EX. 130

EX. 131

Another forward-looking feature is the cadenza-like run with which it ends, and which creates a sense of dynamic instability. Such a device is further heightened by the harmonic mystification at the end of the exposition:

EX. 132

All these features have parallels in the music of Beethoven, whose works are too well known to require quotation here. In many ways, this sonata-allegro of Bach's is like a presynthesis of Beethoven's first pianoforte sonata. Apart from the key, and the opening theme, the triplet writing is very similar to that in the finale of Beethoven's opus 2, no. 1 – especially at the close of the development.

The next two movements are respectively an andante in F major and an 'andantino grazioso' in F minor – an unusual arrangement in view of the absence of a finale in faster tempo. Accompanimental figures in the andante perpetuate the dotted rhythm of the allegro, and take on melodic status later in the movement. The last bars push rhythmic fragmentation, dynamic contrast and harmonic unorthodoxy to the limit:

EX. 133

The 'andantino grazioso' is another movement which invites comparison with the music of later composers. The underlying four-square metrical pulse has echoes in a well-known symphonic march. A subsidiary theme is one of Bach's archetypes:

EX. 134

Compare it with this, taken from the first movement of the fourth of the 'Sonatas with Altered Reprises':

EX. 135

Book IV

The first sonata (G major) in this set is a very slight work, chiefly remarkable for a chain of interesting modulations in the middle movement:

EX. 136

and the fact that the finale is in E major, the key of the rondo which follows and which, in some respects, it resembles.

By contrast, the sonata in E minor is a more substantial composition; but it offers nothing new, the first movement approximating to the style of the 'Sonatas with Altered Reprises' – lyrical, sweet, completely uninspired and the andantino resembling the flowing manner of the rondos. The finale is exclusively composed of dull two-part writing.

Book V

This begins with a sonata in E minor. The opening figure is echoed in a sonata in E flat major by Clementi:

EXX. 137a, b

Clementi shows the better musical judgement in leaving the first beat un-harmonized. The adagio is a short but impressive fantasia, employing some characteristic harmonic features:

EX. 138

In the E major finale, Bach gives us a varied and interesting movement in rondo-style, spiced with striking modulations and richer keyboard writing:

EXX. 139a, b

The composer's grand and altogether more progressive manner re-appears in the fine sonata in B flat which is much more satisfying to play on account of its fuller keyboard texture. The movement is monothematic, and it opens with a heroic gesture:

EX. 140

which inaugurates a rapid triplet sequence leading straight to the double bar. In the recapitulation, EX. 140 is satisfyingly expanded with:

EX. 141

The style of the beautiful largo which follows seems to show the influence of the new school of pianoforte composers – Dusík, Clementi, Hummel and others in its use of octaves:

EX. 142

and the music breathes an altogether more spacious air. Octaves in the finale also give a strong effect towards the end.

Book VI

The first sonata in this book follows a familiar pattern: Scarlatti-type allegro, slow movement (allegretto) and jig-finale. There are rapid contrasts in the opening movement, and a sense of headlong impetus carries the fingers to the final cadence.

In the opening allegretto of the last sonata of the entire collection, Bach compresses a considerable amount of contrasted material into a very short space. This little movement is really a quintessential example of Bach's maturest sonata-style; but one has to be a connoisseur, as Bach himself would insist, to appreciate it. Music of this type presupposes an intimate comprehension of and sympathy with the composer's personal expressive intention. It is not for performance before a huge audience, and the ear which is conditioned by the concert platform cannot be expected to take pleasure in it. In a very literal sense, such music is an intimate communion with the clavichord, and it demands a considerable knowledge of clavichord technique. If we withhold this communion, and judge these works from the standpoint of the pianoforte alone, we shall never attain that degree of connoisseurship to which, in this monumental collection, Emanuel Bach beckons us.

Chapter twelve

The 'Rondos for Connoisseurs and Amateurs'

WITH the rondos we move into a different world. To C. P. E. Bach, the rondo as a musical form is an individual composition standing on its own. Rondo-form is not usually found in the sonatas, and it is obvious from the most cursory examination of both the sonata-finales and the rondos that Bach conceives the rondo as an extended and often lyrical composition. Almost all the rondos in SKL are leisurely works, and almost all are built up around flowing themes. The overall characteristic is a gentle and exquisite refinement. It testifies to a fine-edged musical sensibility, and is more evident than in the first movements of the sonatas; and the reason for this is not hard to find. In the sonata-form movements, as we have seen, we are in the sphere of an emergent tonal dialectic; in the rondos, the dialectical impetus is largely absent. In the absence of dialectical expression, Bach devotes himself mainly to thematic embroidery, and the exploitation of tonal effects without emphasis upon emotional stress.

The abstract rondo-idea, as it is usually presented to students, is symbolized ABACA, where A is a recurring theme and B and C are contrasting thematic episodes. The first and last A's would ideally be in the tonic, B and middle A in the dominant, or other related keys, and C in the subdominant. Other key-variations are of course possible, and these are easy to achieve when the basic form is extended to ABACABA.

But nothing could be more futile than to establish such an idea of rondo-form and then, like Procrustes, look round for examples which fit such an arbitrary conception. This attitude has been the bane of musical textbooks for years. The only idea of value is that a rondo employs a repeated theme and frequently varied and contrasted episodes in related or remote keys. That is how Mozart understood the rondo-concept, and he consistently refused to be bound by arbitrary definitions. Indeed, he frequently blended developmental material with his basic themes and produced his own characteristic forms on a sonata-rondo basis. This type of movement appears in his symphonies. It is almost unanalysable according to conventional schemes.

The rondos of C. P. E. Bach are alike in one important particular; the episodic matter interpolated between statements or variations of the main theme is frequently non-thematic. Rarely does the composer permit the merest snatch of a different melody to hold the stage for more than a second or two. Episodic material consists basically of arpeggiation, sequential passages – sometimes developing an aspect of the theme – and modulating chains of chords which lead to a reprise of the main theme in new keys. In his freely modulating sections, Bach often omits bar-lines, and the result is a temporary compromise with the fantasia-style. This occurs notably in the Rondo in D major (SKL II):

EX. 143

The frequent use of rapid arpeggiation is a very marked feature, and it is present in nearly all the rondos. Generally it breaks out rather unexpectedly, and seems to exist as a self-contained section in the rondo without obvious connecting-links with anything else – unless, as at the end of the Rondo in A minor (SKL II) it is based upon the harmonic structure of the main theme. In such cases, it lends a powerful, climactic emphasis to the theme and enhances the conclusion. In the Rondo in E flat (SKL VI), a variation in running demi-semiquavers like a cadenza is used to round off the composition.

Bach uses the rondo for experimentation in various ways. As in the fantasia, he can exploit tonal effects *ad lib.* without feeling too much bound by the form. This never produces a sense of waywardness; but it is obvious that he enjoys covering a large canvas and, in doing so, exhausting the various possibilities of an idea.

Sometimes, the indwelling dynamic of an idea – an *idea* rather than an obvious melodic inspiration, is very strongly felt. It seems quite clear that the Rondo in A minor (SKL II)[1] exists to justify the juxtaposition of two chords – tonic and diminished seventh – which the very feel of the keyboard invites. Let us follow the vicissitudes of this capricious relationship, which produces music only secondarily, so to speak, as the reflective mind 'catches on' to a train of thought touched off by a satisfying physical sensation in the right hand. Here is the opening theme in full:

EX. 144

It is immediately restated in a varied form, the second phrase X–Y now becoming:

EX. 145

The G natural is an accented passing-note resolving on to the F of the diminished seventh – an imaginative step which enhances the curious fascination of the piece.

Now follows another and more liberal variation:

EX. 146

which is followed by a chromatic passage, crescendo, ending in a full close, piano in C:

EX. 147

After a brief modulation back to A minor, the opening bars of the theme are reversed in C major:

EX. 148

and this is followed by the conventional close as if it were the second half of a full statement of the theme.

Another full statement in A minor, with the second half an octave higher now leads to a chain of modulations:

EX. 149

and to eight bars of arpeggiation as a sequence of sevenths. This ends with the dominant chord of D minor.

The theme reappears in D minor but the full close is displaced by a wedge:

EX. 150

after which there are four bars of arpeggiation and two further statements of the theme, somewhat modified. The second ends abruptly in the tonic, and Bach then recapitulates the arpeggiated series of sevenths, concluding this time with the dominant chord.

The opening two bars are now given more extended treatment:

EX. 151

as are their consequent:

EX. 152

More arpeggiation ushers in a final and dramatic development:

EX. 153

in which every significant version of the opening chords is exploited to the full.

The remainder of the piece consists of a final statement of the example 145, a full and powerful arpeggiation of the whole theme, and four 'farewell bars':

EX. 154

This remarkable composition is a fine example of Bach's fantastic ingenuity, and his economy in wringing music out of virtually nothing. The interest of the piece never decreases, and Bach succeeds in investing his tenuous material with an almost hypnotic power.

It is not always so; there is a limit to what can be achieved on such a slight basis. In the rondo just described, the fascination of the piece grows out of a fertile juxtaposition of two chords – one concordant, the other – by the standards of the day – discordant. But the C major rondo in the same book is a dull work on a dull theme:

EX. 155

A work in similar style to the C major rondo but vastly superior in melodic inspiration and technical organization is the Rondo in E major in SKL III. This, like the work in A minor, is a true connoisseur's piece – leisurely in exposition and development, rich in fascinating detail, at once poetic and precise. The main theme is one of Bach's loveliest melodies:

EX. 156

Particularly happy touches are the natural D and the tied note which are especially appreciated by discerning keyboardists. It is subjected to a great deal of variation, which is well able to stand comparison with Mozart:

EX. 157

There is a follow-on which further explores the nostalgic *Affekt* of the opening melody:

EX. 158

and a further subsidiary motive:

EX. 159

which is obviously extracted from the part-writing of the first bar (see EX. 156).

A feature reminding one of Beethoven is the sharp alternation of *pp* and *ff* in cases like the following, where a soft lyrical flow is broken by an explosive chord followed by a flurry of rapid notes:

EX. 160

This style – in the same key, incidentally – is not unlike that adopted by Beethoven in the first movement of his sonata opus 109. In both works we also find the same kind of broken-chord technique, which is used by Bach both as connecting tissue and as a way of varying the thematic material. Almost all the rondos in SKL employ this device. There is also a similarity of mood between this rondo and the finale of Beethoven's sonata opus 90 in E minor. In the latter work there is the same tendency towards reflective soliloquy and meditative pauses.

Bach's rondo is especially noteworthy for the variety of tonal effects it explores. EX. 160 is an ingenious arrangement of the first four notes in the tenor-line of the first bar of the composition. Most beautiful of all is the change of time and key half-way through the work:

EX. 161

and the subsequent variation of this passage:

EX. 162

After this, the rondo consists mainly of recapitulation, although there are many felicitous touches. I quote the fifth bar from the end. It is worth comparing similar passages at the end of Beethoven's opus 90 with Bach's expressive cadence:

EX. 163

And has Mozart written anything more beautiful than Bach's harmonic and rhythmic variation in the last bar?

EX. 164

Bach never quite achieves the immaculate poise displayed, for example, in Mozart's famous A minor rondo K. 511, but he composes in a comparable manner and his overall achievement in the form is high. It is usual to prescribe K. 511 as an examination-piece for pianoforte diploma candidates. The exquisite grace of Bach's A major rondo in SKL IV would tax their powers just as much, and perhaps permit hitherto undiscovered beauties to break through the stereotyped academic husk of the piano-teacher's humdrum world. It is based upon the following engaging melody:

EX. 165

The second rondo in SKL IV is another piece in E major. It is characterized in the main by rather thin two-part writing on a running theme:

EX. 166

K.M.B.–K

but a beautiful effect is achieved on the basis of a series of modulating chords and syncopations:

EX. 167

The B flat rondo in the same book is based upon a skipping tune:

EX. 168

which subsequently undergoes the following curious treatment:

EX. 169

The C minor rondo in SKL V is a very heterogeneous piece. It is full of hesitations, runs, modulating sequences, and its general effect is more like that of a fantasia. In this piece, there are at least two clearly distinguishable themes, the opening Mannheim arpeggio:

EX. 170

and this, upon which a contrasting middle section is based:

EX. 171

This is quite a different type of work from the other rondos we have discussed. In it, the tension of conflicting elements reappears, and with it Bach's personal brand of enigmatic yet dramatic gesticulation. For instance, after recapitulation of EX. 170 in its tonic key it is violently hurled into F sharp minor, dragged back again as far as E flat minor, and then exploded into a shimmering collocation of arpeggios and triplet scales. One last statement breaks out again before the work ends in a reckless flurry of arpeggiation in C minor – arrested for a moment or two by the neapolitan sixth. The time-space of this work is altogether more densely packed than any of the other rondos. It hovers all the time on the brink of harmonic instability – deliberately contrived to permit the maximum possibility of developmental manoeuvre.

The Rondo in E flat which opens the last volume has a tune more closely resembling the standard conception of what the main melody of a rondo should be. Like the Rondo in C minor, its general texture would have stretched the capacities of Bach's Silbermann clavichord to its utmost. It is quite suitable for fortepiano. Indeed, some of the 'grand effects' employed by Bach now suggest the stronger pianoforte technique being developed by Clementi, Dusík and others:

EX. 172

These mature works of Bach give us a clear idea of what his keyboard performance must have been like. The clavichord is an intimate instrument, its fortissimo is mild compared with that of a harpsichord or piano, but the fact remains that it is not possible to play these rondos successfully upon a pianoforte by striving to emulate the softer tones of the clavichord. They require 'full-bodied' treatment, and can sound brilliantly effective when they are given it. Without falling into Busoni's aberrations, we can safely translate the dynamics of the rondos to the piano keyboard. This will admittedly amplify but not necessarily distort them. Their general texture and style suggest that Bach himself, at the height of his creative and interpretative powers, did not scruple to smite the keys when he felt like doing so. Reducing Bach's texture to a tinkle or a whimper on the piano when he himself probably played with a vigorous attack on his sonorous Silbermann will not help us to enjoy or even understand his music if we are compelled to approach it through the medium of the piano keyboard. However, these remarks are not intended to justify the thoughtless execution of all Bach's music on the piano, but only to temper what has already been said about the intrinsically clavichord music.

And yet the rondo entitled 'A farewell to my Clavichord' is pure clavichord music which absolutely defies adequate interpretation upon the piano. Its most heartfelt moments are enhanced by vibrato, and sound merely banal without it. The main theme is based upon a falling sequential figure. The whole melody falls into two four-bar phrases, the second of which is a filigree variation of the first.

EX. 173

Adventurous modulation is employed throughout, and most characteristic is this series of enharmonic changes which occurs near the end:

EX. 174

Bach wrote this piece when he gave his favourite Silbermann clavichord to his pupil Grotthuss, who responded by composing a rondo entitled 'Joy at receiving the Silbermann Clavier'. This is a cheerful little work but its main interest is that it shows the influence of Emanuel Bach upon a pupil who has listened to his master with one ear, so to speak:

EX. 175a

and tuned into the conventions of eighteenth-century classicism with the other:

EX. 175b

Chapter thirteen

Three Fugues and some miscellaneous pieces

AT the end of this book is a transcript of three fugues (Wotquenne 119/2, 119/4 and 119/6) which Bach composed during the period 1754–63. They afford an interesting insight into Bach's ambivalent attitude to contra- puntal media. Whereas he composes mellifluous counterpoint running serenely along dignified but somewhat stereotyped tracks in the fugues in A and E flat, the D minor piece achieves a lively effect by the simple a-contrapuntal device of broken chords. One feels that in Emanuel's day fugues were still very much associated with learning rather than inspira- tion, with a self-conscious academicism rather than fluent expression. Indeed, Marpurg added analytical comments to the text of the A major fugue, so that the performer can enjoy the systematic demonstration of contrapuntal devices as he plays. In both the A major and E flat fugues he numbered the bars. The E flat is a long composition of 250 bars.

I suggested in Chapter three that it was not good enough to regard Emanuel's fugues merely as examples of his indifference to the instru- mental fugue. We have it on Burney's authority that Bach was devoted to his father's fugues, and was a profound exponent of the *Well-Tempered Clavier*; and it seems to me that his own examples are sufficiently enjoy- able as music to justify reprinting them. It is not difficult to imagine C. P. E. Bach playing both his father's and his own fugues with great technical refinement, and with close attention to a singing style of per- formance. The A major piece certainly invites a leisurely *cantando* per- formance, and it will repay practice. More importantly, Bach occasion- ally resorted to fugal methods in his sonatas. The sonata in F minor (Wotquenne 62/6) composed *circa* 1744 is a fine, rugged composition, and the first movement achieves its impressive effect in virtue of the interplay of its two subjects. One wishes Bach had ventured more in this style, which somewhat anticipates the mood of a Beethoven sonatina in the same key:

EX. 176

This piece appeared first in *Musikalisches Allerley* in 1761, and was subsequently reprinted by Farrence in his *Le Trésor de Pianistes*.

When enjoying the dramatic interplay of conflicting elements in the sonatas, and delighting in the elegance and melodiousness of Emanuel's lighter compositions, it is all too easy to overlook a persistent feature of his style. This oversight arises from a fallacious historical judgement, and the refusal to apply analytical insight to compositions which do not immediately seem to demand it. When discussing and analysing fugues, it is natural to look for inversion, diminution, augmentation, stretto and the like, and the conception of a long composition growing from some germinal thematic idea seems too familiar to require special comment. When, on the other hand, we turn to compositions in a simpler, homophonic style, consisting basically of a tuneful theme, a few simple extensions and an almost rudimentary accompaniment, it may never occur to us to look for precisely the same structural conception. It often seems to me that we have somewhat overplayed the notion that eighteenth-century keyboard music is in reaction against the contrapuntal structures of the baroque era. Once we begin to examine the details of Emanuel Bach's seemingly inconsequential structures with a more analytical ear, many interesting features are revealed. We find, for example, that he delights in turning simple motivic fragments inside out, and in building up complete sentences simply by taking up different standpoints in relation to some primary harmonic or thematic idea. An interval may yield the richest results simply by appearing simultaneously as a thematic and harmonic unit, and this can happen just as much in a simple homophonic composition as in a fugue. Instead, then, of considering music from a specifically contrapuntal or harmonic angle, as if these two positions are mutually exclusive, we should direct our analytical attention to the synthesis, and look for the unifying motival element which reveals both harmonic and melodic features as aspects of a single idea.

This way of considering Emanuel's work invites us to relate all his music to the tradition represented by his father. Instead, then, of seeing Emanuel merely as an innovator reacting violently against tradition (the traditional textbook picture), we see him as an innovator still subconsciously motivated by many compositional ideas which are almost as old as music itself. It is an interesting question how far a composer whose compositions reveal an inner thematic unity is deliberately manipulating a key idea and how far he is subconsciously taking up different emotional standpoints in relation to that idea. Be that as it may, a glance at the A major fugue reveals the extent to which Emanuel Bach mastered the contrapuntal art. Following this, an examination of some of his lighter pieces will show how he employed unifying thematic and harmonic devices in the composition of quite different textures. The point is that a single creative mind was at work in both instances. We have already noticed in discussion of the sonatas that different movements are sometimes quite obviously bound together by some unifying idea. This fact does not, of course, over-ride the principle of contrast and opposition, either between separate movements which exhibit a common thematic motivation, or within a single movement where a fragment is treated in different ways. One might say that whereas, in a fugue, different *structural* orientations are demonstrated by subjecting a theme to inversion, diminution and retrograde progression, a sonata reveals different *emotional* orientations. This principle remains true whether a movement is obviously monothematic, or whether it is built up from contrasting fragments, and whether the basic material is treated homophonically or contrapuntally.

The subject of the A major fugue is worth considering in some detail, because a close familiarity with all its implications at once reveals Emanuel's fantastic ingenuity in developing it throughout the entire composition. It breaks down into three main phrases, A descending to E scalewise, then the series F sharp, C sharp, D sharp, E, suggesting a modulation to the dominant, and finally another scalewise descent which concludes the subject in the tonic. Undoubtedly, Schenker and Katz would see this subject as a precise statement of the harmonic relationship I-V-I, the D sharp conventionally implying modulation but in fact only enhancing transition through the dominant. A further point of some interest is that the first two phrases are each enclosed by a perfect fourth. Obviously a subject of this kind is rich in structural potential, and no single fugue based upon it could do more than unravel a limited number of its possibilities. Even so, Bach does very well. Almost every bar of this composition reveals a linear progression in one part or another derived from the thematic motivation of the subject. Bar 6, to take an example near the beginning, shows two groups of quavers, the first echoing the first four notes of the subject in diminution, the second imitating the second four by diminution and reverse motion.

Given a conjunct subject like this one, which can be subdivided into three phrases, it is a simple matter to construct varied linear patterns by altering the pitch relationships between them and exploring the permutations which result by making them follow one another in different orders. This gives rise to long, flowing passages which are always en-joyable to play on a keyboard instrument.

The subject is initially answered by a tonal version of the theme which balances the original modulation to the dominant by an implicit affirma-tion of the tonic. Conversely, however, the subject falls to the dominant note as the harmony is stabilized in time for a tonic entry of the third voice. Some special features of Bach's subsequent treatment of his material are worth pointing out. Beginning in bar 28 we have a long episode by diminution, retrograde and inverse movement being employed to demon-strate different forms of the motivic fragments making up the subject. Bar 35 initiates a strong sequence with reinforcing octaves in the bass which give prominence to the first four notes of the theme as the upper parts chatter in quaver patterns reminiscent of the basic thematic figuration. At bar 55 another sequential episode explores the possibilities of diminution, retrograde and contrary development of phrase two of the subject of the fugue; and at bar 70 we have a sequence of perfect fifths in the accompaniment which may well have given the composer an idea for the fugue in E flat. Preoccupied with such devices, the disguised augmented entry at bar 45 may well escape notice. The canon at bar 80 is introduced by a statement of the subject which is accompanied by figuration derived by diminution and inversion from its second phrase. A further canonic extension beginning at bar 101, and based this time upon full but diminished versions of the subject, introduces a final *tour de force* in which diminished statements of the subject, following one another in rapid succession, are sounded against the original theme. Bars 115–17 hint again at the subject of the E flat fugue.

The fugue in E flat should silence at once any critics who may suggest that the master of *Empfindsamkeit* was not disciplined in the contrapuntal art. It is an intense, closely-reasoned composition in which no conces-sions whatever are made to facile melodic patterns. Whereas the A major fugue is based upon obvious linear progressions, this one is derived from the harmonic implications of its severely uncompromising subject, and the composer builds up massive harmonic structures in the performance of which a player unused to such intellectual rigours can easily lose his way.

The crotchets accompanying the tonal answer seem at first as if they are going to turn into a regular counter-subject; but this does not materialize. Even so, this crotchet pattern yields scalic figures which reappear frequently in the unfolding texture. There are, in any case, other interesting features which claim attention. Not the least of these is the emergence of a loose double fugue at bar 47 on what sound like two new subjects. Both, however, show thematic relationships with the counterpoint which first appears under the tonal answer (bar 5 *et seq.*).

Another point worth noting is that the long descent in slow notes in the upper part at bar 47 sounds like a memory of the subject of the fugue in A major as well as an augmentation of the lower part in bars 6 and 7. Yet again, the theme given out in the alto beginning at bar 48 has an identical rhythm with the disguised entry at bar 45 in the A major fugue. These cross-references, possibly incidental, are interesting because they suggest that the use of unifying motivic fragments by a composer may be largely unconscious. At bar 72 the original subject is integrated with the slow descending figure of the double fugue, and another theme is added in the uppermost part. This is not systematically worked out although echoes of it persist in fragments for many bars at a time. Analysis will reveal that this new figure is built up from simple elements which will be found in the subject of the A major fugue. Towards the end, the fugue is gathered together in portentous passages in which stretto devices play a leading part, and the composition is closed on a tonic pedal.

Considered overall, the fugue in E flat is a highly abstract and intellectual work offering, perhaps, more food for the head than for the heart. But as an essay in the functions of counterpoint and the growth of organic tonal structure from severely archetypal beginnings, it is highly satisfying, and a not inconsiderable achievement. The more one learns, from study and experience, about the nature of musical thinking, the more respect one feels for a composer who can discover the thought embedded even in the most rudimentary material. This book is primarily concerned with musical forms which have arisen from a predominantly expressionist aesthetic; but feeling, as Bach well knew, is not enough, and it is important to be able to think with sounds. That such thinking often seems like the discovery of something already hidden or enfolded in a melodic fragment or an interval is a mystery apprehended, if not fully comprehended, by every true musician. Everyone is familiar with the wonderful forms revealed by the microscope. A composer of fugues is, in effect, subjecting a formal arrangement of tones to a microscopic analysis, and revealing some of the beauties hidden therein.

The fugue in D minor is in quite a different style. Like the others it is a closely-reasoned composition; but the initial theme offers no analytical problems, and the body of the fugue unfolds with transparent logic from the subject. Moreover, the simple construction in two parts makes it an easy work to enjoy at the keyboard. There are recurring patterns of figuration, frequent inversions and altogether the fugue seems to take fuller account of the specific tendencies of keyboard technique in the eighteenth century than the two works already discussed.

As previously indicated, one of the most valuable collections of C. P. E. Bach's keyboard pieces available today is the volume entitled *Kurze und leichte Klavierstücke*. Indeed, one does not need to look farther for a demonstration of Bach's genius in the smaller, lyrical forms, although, as we shall see, there are many other individual compositions worthy of notice. The editor of the *Wiener Urtext Ausgabe* suggests that this collection stands in much the same relation to keyboard technique as J. S. Bach's two- and three-part Inventions – the implication being, presumably, that whereas one might practise the Inventions to gain a mastery in the performance of baroque textures, Emanuel's pieces could be studied in relation to late eighteenth-century keyboard techniques. Obviously this is a valid point, because the *Kurze und leichte Klavierstücke* are subtitled *mit veränderten Reprisen und beigefügter Fingersetzung für Anfänger*. These pieces give instruction in the art of composition and in fingering. It is especially interesting that Emanuel could conceive these two aspects of musicianship in such a close relationship. This, like so many other factors in his work, reveals an integrated musical consciousness. How many modern music teachers discern or presuppose any integral connection between fingering techniques and the structure of musical thought?

As a general principle, these pieces with varied reprises reveal the remarkable extent to which Emanuel Bach derived musical structures from simple unifying elements. His procedure is to begin with a short melodic statement, and then subject it to melodic variation, sometimes with ornamental patterns of increasing complexity. It has already been pointed out in connection with the Sonatas with Altered Reprises that such ornamentation is not merely something added to a tune. At its most significant it is drawn out of a primary tonal relationship. What is even more interesting, and this is a fact which can easily escape the notice of a casual investigator, is that the primary material itself reveals a remarkable unity of structure, in that both melodic and accompanying parts derive from a single chord or an elementary linear progression. A point to bear in mind, then, whilst playing these delightful little compositions, is that the first generating statement is a storehouse of motivic relations, and each varied reprise is a further revelation of their logical implications. What we observe, in effect, is something similar to the technique employed in the fugue in A major abstracted from a rigorous contrapuntal context, and exhibited with an exquisite lucidity in simple textures. To play these works is to be instructed in composition, to learn how to use the resources logically enfolded in the simplest material, to be disciplined in structural economy. Above all, it is to realize that the art of music is itself a unity, and to become suspicious of sharp distinctions, guillotines and watersheds in the written history of music.

Schenker has already analysed the first piece, and the graph he made of it is conveniently reproduced in the *Wiener Urtext Ausgabe*. I would refer the reader especially to the ninth piece in the set, an 'Andante e sostenuto' which is surely one of the most beautiful two-part inventions ever composed. It is only sixteen bars long, and it is so closely worked, and so homogeneous in conception, that quotation could serve no useful purpose. Oswald Jonas supplies a graph of the piece in his editorial comments which explains its harmonic basis as a series of broken chords and reveals many points of interest. There are also other features which require comment. The first eight notes in the melodic part (d–b flat–f sharp–a–g–f natural–e flat–d) supply three motivic fragments. These are d–b flat–f sharp, b flat–f sharp–a–g, and a–g–f natural–e flat–d. All are telescoped into one another in the first bar, yet they appear separately and in a variety of permutations throughout the rest of the piece, the melodic structure being almost entirely derived from them. This derivation takes the form of a continuous arioso, broken with affecting little sighs, some almost magical chromatic alterations and an infallible sense of line. In playing this work, one realizes how much performance depends, in truth, upon musical insight into texture, and how closely thought and feeling are bound together. The outwardness of the object and the inwardness of one's response to it seem to be two sides of the same penny. How easy it is to forget this, or to deny it in the name of mere technical proficiency! The result can only be a denigration of the musical consciousness.

Not all the compositions in this collection demonstrate such intimate thematic and harmonic relationships as the piece just described; but enough has been said to direct the interested pianist to a scrutiny of Emanuel's methods and procedures, even in seemingly slight compositions which appear not to require analytical investigation. Particularly pleasing works are the Arioso in C (number 2 in the set), Alla Polacca (number 5), Allegretto (number 6) and the Allegro and Allegretto (numbers 19 and 20).

C. P. E. Bach frequently employs the principle of the varied reprise in many other compositions without drawing special attention to the fact in the title. It is, of course, almost indigenous to his melodic style. Haydn adopts it in many a keyboard work, and through him it passes into the classical Viennese tradition.

Chivalry, and the belief, now almost dead in these days of feminine emancipation, that ladies of refinement should be specially provided for at the keyboard, probably inspired Emanuel to compose his sonatas *à l'usage des Dames*. They are interesting because they show Bach applying the resources of his musical maturity to light-weight sonatas of a diversionary nature. According to the long and involved title, which includes a fulsome reference to the composer's professional position at Hamburg, these works are 'pour le Clavecin'. In my opinion, this designation should not be taken too seriously. The sonatas unmistakably, and particularly in the slow movements, show the affecting cadences characteristic of Emanuel's clavichord style. No doubt they were played on the harpsi-chord by the society ladies who could afford one; but there are passages which gain immeasurably from a clavichord performance. This is very much the case with the first sonata, which seems to anticipate in the themes and working-out section of its first movement a sonata in F by Mozart (K.547a) for violin and piano, subsequently transcribed for pianoforte solo. It is unusual to find Bach breaking off into recitative at the end of a strongly rhythmical allegro. He does so here, however, and indulges in a series of dramatic, enharmonic modulations which make a completely unexpected coda to the movement. One might, indeed, be excused for feeling that the demanding contrasts of tone and the heavy-handedness implied by the written notation are positively masculine in their assertiveness. The sonata is in two movements, the second being a satisfyingly worked-out structure in six-eight time embodying varied repetitions.

Other sonatas in the set combine an appealing lyrical sensitivity with structural devices of great subtlety. The second sonata has a lovely little slow movement with varied repetition of the opening theme, and its finale demonstrates the structural economy of a simple broken chord technique. The third begins with a 'harmonic' theme which is immediately varied. The rest of the first movement is a clever development of motivic elements which seem to be suggested by the bass figure in the eighth bar. Another point to observe is the immense rhythmic variety of the piece. The remaining pieces in the set have much to offer the pianist, and special mention should be made of the beautiful little siciliano in the fourth sonata, the slow movement of the fifth, and the sixth sonata in its entirety. The *Damensonaten* contain much beautiful and readily accessible music. At the same time, they demand much more in the way of imaginative interpretation than the often mechanical sonatinas of Muzio Clementi with which young pianists are frequently plagued. A special point in their favour which would make them extremely valuable for young students is their lyricism. Some movements have a melodic richness and grace which are not found in the proliferating albums of 'early classics' which are sometimes a student's only introduction to eighteenth-century keyboard music, and this is a great stimulus to the development of mature connoisseurship. It is still, unfortunately, possible to pass as a 'qualified music teacher' without having the least idea how to make musical sense of works like these. One remembers Emanuel's earnest injunction: 'Play from the soul, not like a trained bird' (Mitchell translation of the *Versuch*, p. 150). A great barrier to the development of a richer musical life in Britain in the twentieth century is a continued ignorance of the inner spirit and motivation of much of the music which delighted eighteenth-century musicians, and an unreflective acceptance of a mechanical system of musical education. Such a system seems to leave no room for feeling and expression, whereas practical technique and 'paper-work' are taught in dry abstraction from the living tissue of musical thought. It is necessary to emphasize this point because here and there voices are raised in protest against musicologists who seem to be too much concerned with 'history'. A true insight into musical history is the life-blood of musical experience.

In addition to the sonatas composed for ladies of refinement, many individual representatives of the fair sex are honoured in Emanuel Bach's works. Upwards of twenty programmatic little compositions bear a lady's name. Amongst these are some delightful little musical portraits – *La Gleim, La Bergius, La Prinzette, La Louise, La Gabriel*. Some of these pieces are highly original compositions, and they are written in different styles and forms. *La Lott*, for instance, is a stately minuet, and it is included (although without its title) in the album published by the Universal Edition (No. 11015 – piece number 5). *L'Auguste* is a polonaise and it will also be found, along with *La Sybille, La Xenophon* and *La Capricieuse* in U.E. 11015. But perhaps the most impressive feminine portrait is *La Stahl*. This is in effect a tragic *scena*, abounding in plangent harmonies and impassioned recitative:

EX. 177

It is reported (by Geiringer)[1] that the sad demeanour of this lady derived from the loss of her children. At any rate, Bach lavished some fine music upon her, and outside the fantasias and sonatas it is one of the best examples of his expressive, declamatory style. The work is mono-thematic in construction, and a notable feature is the flattened supertonic (E flat), twice repeated in the opening bars, which plays an important part afterwards. An apparently new theme introduced after the double bar is obviously derived from the opening statement. Anyone with an interest in human reactions will wonder what the lady felt when Emanuel played this powerful little tone-poem to her. One is also led to speculate about the character of *La Caroline*, who is introduced with a delicious theme in A minor, 'Allegro ma con tenerezza'!

La Stahl, in D minor, would make an excellent prelude to the scintillating set of harpsichord variations on *La Follia*, which is in the same key. Both pieces are reprinted in Peters Edition 4188. Not all the variations are of equal value; but special mention should be made of number 3, which achieves a magnificent and modern-sounding effect in virtue of 'wrong notes' subtly inserted into the arpeggiation:

EX. 178

Variation V is also striking. The bass figure is pursued remorselessly to the final cadence:

EX. 179

and variation II has a brooding atmosphere of repressed power.

Amongst sundry other lighter pieces, the Allegro in E and the Allegro in C major are especially attractive (see Peters Edition 4188). The E major is a pleasing, well-rounded composition in classical style with a balanced ritornello/concertante flow, and the C major, also a rondo, is really a study for the right hand:

EX. 180

There are a number of other pieces, including fantasias, marches, dances in various rhythms, solfeggi and a curious little piece which is for the practice of either hand alone, written on one stave. *Les Langeurs Tendres* evokes the spirit of Couperin and Rameau not only in its title but also in its manner:

EX. 181

The many minuets frequently anticipate Haydn's style, and they include a number of delightful and poetic miniatures. The following piece comes from the *Kurze und leichte Stücke* and is also reprinted in a shortened form in the Chester album:

EX. 182

The varied reprises in this little work exploit a vein of lyrical rhapsody which it seems unusual to find in a work composed so many years before Chopin's mazurkas. Bearing in mind Emanuel Bach's long experience of the clavichord, the development of the piano in his later years, and his own avowed concentration upon a singing style of performance, it is possible to trace a line of evolution in his musical thinking which almost by-passes the classical era to enter the sphere of romanticism. In Weber's beautiful pianoforte sonata in A flat, for example, there are many lovely moments which seem like enhancements, in terms of romantic pianism, of elements already present in C. P. E. Bach's slow movements. One would not wish to press such an apparently enthusiastic claim too far. At the same time, no one who gains an intimate insight into Emanuel's smaller pieces will deny that a romantic poet lurked under the pre-classical exterior.

The poetry of this little minuet in A major will also bring grace and beauty to a recreative moment:

EX. 183

From the standpoint of the clavier-player, an interesting and unexpected light is thrown upon Bach's keyboard style by the accompaniments to his *Spiritual Songs*.[2] Of these, there are at least one hundred and eighty. There is an album of thirty in Peters Edition. In most cases, the melodic line is written into the keyboard part, and so the accompaniments are virtually little keyboard pieces. Although it is doubtless undesirable to regard them in this way, the fact remains that they stand performance on their own – as songs without words. Particularly beautiful, when performed as pianoforte solos, are the *Passionslied, Bitten,*

Prüfung am Abend and *Abendlied* – all from Gellert's Odes. In these pieces we see the same characteristic figuration, the same affecting sighs, the nostalgic phraseology, the hesitations, lyrical recitative and ornamentation as we find in the slow movements of many sonatas. In fact, it seems highly likely that the serious, ruminating vein of such movements owes not a little to the composer's religious sensibility. We should be wrong to attribute the inspiration of the instrumental works to an exclusively secular expressionism. The following fragment has many echoes in the sonatas:

EX. 184 (*Abendlied*)

It is worth remembering that one of the ancestors of the solo clavier sonata was the *sonata da chiesa* originally for strings with continuo and then taken over by Kuhnau for the clavichord. Again, if Bach, in his keyboard works, frequently looks forward to Beethoven, have not these spiritual songs, with their deeply felt accompaniments, an organic connection with the more serious songs of Beethoven and Brahms?

It is important to distinguish between works for solo keyboard with which we have been mainly concerned, and which reveal the innermost aspiration of the composer, and the many concertos and chamber works requiring keyboard *continuo* or *solo*. The earlier concertos are characterized by *baroque* traces and *galant* elements; but the later works are remarkably expansive pieces employing thematic contrast and harmonic audacity to a considerable extent. Emanuel Bach's mature compositions in this genre are true forerunners of Beethoven's concerto-style. They have a classical expansiveness and fully worked-out symphonic developments. However, a thorough analytical discussion of these interesting compositions will be included in another book devoted to a comprehensive survey of Emanuel's life and work.

Chapter fourteen

A final appraisal

WE have surveyed the most important keyboard music of Emanuel Bach, relating it to the aesthetic theories of his day and his own expressed convictions, tracing connexions between the fantasia and the sonata, following the threads of musical expression from its unfettered outpourings in improvisation to its higher discipline and organization by the sonata-principle, and relating this growth to the metaphysical principle which found diverse expression in the latter days of the eighteenth century.

This study has been undertaken in the light of a conviction strongly held; namely that the growth of a style, a form, an aesthetic theory can always be related to some universal factor which may, or may not, be made explicit in the philosophy of the time, but which will certainly be apparent to the mind which is disposed to synthesis rather than the fragmentation of human experience.

If it be objected that this *Gestalt* outlook, this pre-disposition to integrate apparently disparate factors within a comprehensive viewpoint, is out of place, my reply is that history is in a special sense 'the unconscious mind' of our present consciousness. To understand the musical procedures of the past today, we must realize that they express factors underpinning our present musical apprehension. And as our own consciousness is contiguous with the present and past of the infinite variety of human experience, so our musical understanding cannot ultimately be separated from our deepest intuition of the hidden energies of the history of philosophical thought. And finally, any principle of explanation which makes sense of a complex historical phenomenon has to be considered on its merits, and must stand as a valid hypothesis until disproved.

In the case of C. P. E. Bach's keyboard music we have a musical phenomenon which is directly relatable to the philosophy of its time – a philosophy which had repercussions in the other arts, and latterly even in the political world. In the beginning, this philosophy took its stand upon the imitation of nature. Notwithstanding C. F. Cramer's objection:[1]

'In Nature there are no leaps; changes do not occur through sudden shifts of direction; no feeling suddenly yields to its opposite.'

the Berlin theorists, and Bach among them, based their musical philosophy of ebb and flow upon what they believed to be a natural phenomenon subjectively apprehended.

An amusing and happy confirmation of the Berlin aesthetic comes from an unexpected quarter. In 1779 Dr Anton Mesmer published his historic *Memoire sur la Découverte du Magnétisme Animal*. In this, he formulated his doctrine of animal magnetism in twenty-seven propositions. It affirms that there is a universal 'fluid' permeating all things, which determines the properties of Matter and the Organic Body, and that this fluid is characterized by two polarities, like a magnet, generating alternate effects, reciprocal Ebb and Flow (Propositions 2 and 3). This universal agent insinuates itself into the human organism through the nerves, where its alternating polarities are first felt, and through the medium of which they are subjectively apprehended. It is tempting to speculate upon possible connexions, hidden in the unconscious mind, between the psychophysical phenomena classified by Mesmer and the theory of *Empfindsamkeit*.

Be that as it may, we have to remember that apart from the official doctrine of the Church, Europe and Germany in particular, in Bach's day, were very much concerned with the investigation of the human soul. The basic problem which occupied philosophers, the respectable academic ones like Kant as well as the less familiar occultists like Karl von Eckartshausen, concerned the relation and interaction between Mind and Matter, the subjective stuff of the soul and the objective stuff of which the outside world was made.

Practical concern with this problem came very close indeed to C. P. E. Bach during his twenty-eight years at the Prussian Court, for King Frederick Wilhelm himself (to whom Bach dedicated four symphonies) was something of a dabbler in the occult and a regular visitor at 'The House of Evocation' in Berlin which he subsequently owned. It is said that Frederick was regularly present at this haunt of necromancy when the souls of the dead were evoked! I mention this only to indicate how speculation about music and its subjective inspiration was encompassed about by other significant factors in the mental life of the time. The solution of the mind-matter problem in academic philosophy was by way of synthesis, and of course it was Hegel who overcame the aesthetic of nature-imitation by asserting the dialectical principle. This principle at once brings together the natural and the spiritual world in a dynamic unity, self-established by a rational procedure of opposition and synthesis.

I suggest that as the nature of the supreme synthesis was philosophically grasped, it also demonstrated itself in music. Hegel's insight is not a merely abstract notion, although it may be inconceivably remote from the common apprehension. It is a mode of understanding which is accessible to the highest aspirations of the creative impulse. Having clearly formulated the antithesis of mind and matter, and having recognized the persistence of polarity even within the subjective consciousness as well as the multiplicity of phenomena in the outside world, a synthetic philosophy was ultimately inevitable.

Likewise, having once sanctioned the reality of the interior life, having accepted the passion of the soul as the *prima materia* of musical inspiration, the eventual establishment of the sonata-principle was a necessity – not as Marxians envisage necessity, but as Plato and Plotinus envisage it, as a crowning phase of intellectual insight substantiating a new and profounder experience.

The formal synthesis was really achieved by Beethoven. As far as the sonata-principle was concerned, and the subjective drive which it disciplined by a rational, objective procedure, the nineteenth century could do little but applaud the Viennese victory. It is rather pathetic to see Mahler armed with a huge orchestra, arriving at the battlefield eighty years later, and (in an almost literal sense) having nothing but corpses to fight against. Mahler experienced his own antitheses and tried to win through to a new synthesis. But he only parodied the earlier history of the sonata-principle. Because his main inspirations were lyrical rather than dialectical, his long hymns in praise of the symphonic word of unity are less convincing than the sonatas of Emanuel Bach.

Bach struggled to idealize and unify his inspiration. 'Idealize' means here to exalt the subjective standpoint by an expressionist theory of musical values. 'Unify' means to bring an objective tonal order to birth which coheres through the strength of its own interior structure. As we have seen, this struggle created a compelling intensity.

At the same time, we must recognize that the very tenacity with which Bach and his contemporaries clung to the aesthetic of *Empfindsamkeit* tended to hinder their development beyond a certain point. To cling to a theory of subjective expressionism is to polarize one's inspiration on the subjective side, to build a theoretical fence around one's inspiration. This, from the standpoint of an historical phase, may well be 'necessary', since the eventual formulation of an objective rational order must always depend upon a vigorous subjective affirmation. Theoretically considered, Emanuel Bach is thus a subjective 'moment' in the emergent synthesis, necessary to the historical manifestation of a tonal concept.

Whatever the truth of the matter, it does seem as if Bach gave himself to an idea. Devotion to subjective expression resulted in an intimate and personal style, frequently of very great beauty. But we cannot fruitfully deny that his melodies are often 'short-winded', that a moment of genuine feeling often seems to exhaust inspiration for a time, that the self-generation of a motive for composition leads to the curious juxtaposition of profundity and triteness, that the curling *Manieren* of a lovely phrase are not always a sufficient justification of thin textures and feeble harmonic progressions, and that harmonic audacity must always be balanced by a satisfying control of more orthodox procedures.

What is sometimes a source of disappointment in C. P. E. Bach is the sparse and unsatisfactory way he deals with melody and figuration requiring at least a good basis of solid, conventional filling-up. The occasional lack of this will always be a bar to his wider appreciation.

It is easy, of course, to see how this 'thin-ness' arises. From the fugues in A and E flat, and the baroque-like textures of some movements in the 'Prussian' and 'Württemberg' sonatas, it is perfectly obvious that Bach could handle a rich texture adequately. But like all initiates into the art of musical composition, he knew that whereas contrapuntal and serialized procedures are an acceptable guarantee of musical learning in the eyes of the uninitiated, they are all too easy a standby in the absence of a real creative impulse. Even today, we feel that a modern composer who ends his *magnum opus* with a fugue must be a composer indeed.

Bach deliberately and consistently chose to avoid the conventional answer to his tonal problems. When contrapuntal textures were required, as in the oratorio *Israel in der Wüste*, then he provided them. But in the fantasias, and sonatas, he chose the harmonic conflict, the thematic variety, and when no obvious figure of accompaniment suggested itself, he relied upon thin two-part textures, or arpeggios, or even unaccompanied melody and figuration enhanced solely by *Bebung*, retardations and contrasting dynamics. In this he shows a commendable aesthetic integrity, a readiness to explore an experimental manner to the full in accordance with his new artistic creed. We should not censure him for not composing in a manner he consciously eschewed.

The modern clavichordist or pianist who explores Emanuel's keyboard work has a twofold task. He has to discover the mental and spiritual *nisus* of his musical inspiration as a pre-requisite for reliving and interpreting his music. If he chooses to play the best works before an audience of connoisseurs, then upon him will fall the mantle of *Empfindsamkeit*. He will have to play as if he means it, and not with the slick efficiency of a pianist trained on post-eighteenth-century techniques. If he chooses to play only for himself, he will be able to relive and rediscover the fundamental polarities of the musical consciousness which gave birth to the most fertile principle of musical thinking which history has produced.

The sonatas of Emanuel Bach, embedded as they are in an attitude to music which requires great imaginative penetration on the part of the interpreter, are an invitation to the musical mind to broaden its background awareness of the deep and often hidden elements which leavened the eighteenth-century mind. If we are to place Emanuel Bach somewhere on the scale defined by the polarities of sensuous beauty and intellectual abstraction, we shall have to admit that we are dealing with a mind of considerable intellectual subtlety. This may lead us to the view that Emanuel Bach was primarily a theorist who consciously manipulated his effects with a cold appraisal of their impact upon the listener. Circumstantial evidence of Bach's general character might give some support to this view. For example, for a man who placed such emphasis upon emotion and feeling, he seems to have displayed singularly little sentiment in the way he treated his father's widow, or in the way he disposed of the engraved plates of *The Art of Fugue*.[2]

Was Bach, then, a cold musical intellect, manifesting a detached connoisseurship, calculating his effects and inclining always to the polarity of intellectual abstraction?

I do not think so. The element of intellectual abstraction is certainly there in his music, and it is strong; but against it we have the undoubtedly sensuous and affecting beauty of many of his clavichord compositions. We also have Burney's testimony which affirms his inspired playing, his power in expressive improvisation, the rapt introspection which made him oblivious to the passage of time. As I see it, Emanuel Bach was an intellectual musician in whom the fires of inspiration burned at a deep level. These were fanned by an intellectual affirmation of musical expressionism and called forth by a strong will. His introspective nature inclined him especially to the clavichord. We can well imagine Bach slipping away after a tedious session of continuo playing, in which he accompanied King Frederick through some interminable batch of flute concertos by Quantz, to the privacy of his own quarters, there to commune with himself in a rhapsodic stream of improvisation and fantasy. His finest keyboard effects are a direct outgrowth of his improvisatory genius. His theory of modulation and expression is a rationalization of what in him was instinctive and inspirational. No man can devote himself to an idea unless that idea beckons to something fundamental in his own nature.

I imagine that Emanuel's clavichord music will similarly beckon to introspective keyboardists who have the tenacity, the historical imagination and the theoretical insight which will encourage them to consider it in the deeper context of late eighteenth-century thought. They will find that the creative tensions of a bygone age can spring into life through straining fingers and a probing imagination.

C. P. E. Bach's views on performance with some practical suggestions

MANY contemporary observers paid tribute to Emanuel's keyboard performance, and it is unnecessary to repeat these tributes here. William Mitchell quotes the most important reports in his introduction to the English edition of the *Essay*. It is interesting to consider the composer's own views on performance and to take note of some of their implications. Apart from this, the performance of his music upon a modern pianoforte raises some problems, and as many readers of this book will have no other instrument within easy reach, a few suggestions may not be amiss.

Some preliminary observations are necessary. In general, there are two main trends in musicology. One is the discovery and publication of manuscripts in modern performing versions. The other is the establishment of the correct ways of playing old music. One frequently suspects that when every ornament has been properly interpreted and faithfully rendered, when every instrument tallies with the one indicated in the score, when scholarship and a zealous regard for antiquities have done their utmost (one is sometimes tempted to put it more strongly) – that when all has been done, the music fails to make a 'break-through'.

In some way culture and scholarship fail. Or is the listener wrong for expecting more than a distorted version of the original? Is the original a kind of idealistic myth, impossible to realize? In familiar terms, it seems to be a matter of the relationship between head and heart, mind and spirit, tone and the innermost creative dynamic. In so many cases, when the technical aspect of performance seems impeccable, the spirit is dead.

An interesting question arises: what subtle inter-relationships are there between the technique of composition and the manner of performance? In the case of some composers, the *manner* of extemporaneous performance stimulated and underpinned a definite manner of composition. Delius is a well-known case. Prolonged harmonic rhapsody at the piano, only loosely bound by melodic threads is obviously the basis of his compositional style in all media.

We have already considered Emanuel Bach's manner at the keyboard in respect of improvisation and fantasia. We have further considered the emergence of the integral principle in his musical thought, the importance of synthesis, the assertion of unity in and through conflicting polarities, the hidden motivic unity which is sometimes revealed in his works. This integral principle, we have suggested, is not limited to music. The principle of unity in variety is a dialectical principle with universal applications. In the performance of Bach's sonatas, should we be alive to all the mental factors involved? In what sense could the emergent aesthetic of the sonata-principle, as distinct from the generalized factor of expressive playing, be expected to condition our attitude at the keyboard?

When we consider Emanuel's own words, in the chapter on Performances in the *Essay*, these questions seem quite important.[1] No final answer can be given; but a general attitude emerges which we must note.

Bach has not much use for keyboardists 'whose chief asset is technique' (p. 147 in Mitchell's translation). They are at a disadvantage, especially so – the author might have added – when they try to play *his* music. Furthermore, 'it is only rarely possible to reveal the true content and affect of a piece on its first reading' (p. 147), although sight-reading is 'a commendable ability' (p. 147). Bearing in mind Bach's almost neurotic dread of boring performance, which 'gives us no choice but to slumber' (p. 148) – a fear expressed on more than one occasion in the *Essay*, it is not surprising to find him advocating the following vital principle:

'. . . a stirring performance depends upon an alert mind which is willing to follow reasonable precepts in order to reveal the content of compositions' (p. 148).

One remembers Liszt's famous injunction to think twenty times and play once.

Good performance depends upon:

'the ability through singing or playing to make the ear conscious of the true content and affect of a composition' (p. 148)

and upon the proper recognition of forte and piano, legato and staccato, vibrato, arpeggiation, retardation and accelerando, and most importantly upon playing all notes and their embellishments in correct time 'with fitting volume produced by a touch which is related to the true content of a piece'.

'Play from the soul,' urges Bach, 'not like a trained bird' (p. 150).

Listen to soloists and ensembles, and develop your own sensibility thereby.

We may observe at once that more than one great pianist has given this or similar advice. This is not surprising, because every real musician, as distinct from the mere manipulator, knows that the act of performance is a creative act, and that, in the act of creation, an 'outside' medium, in this case tone, is informed by imaginative subjective generation.

A work only exists – as far as this world is concerned – during the time of its performance. In what sense it can be said to exist when it is not being performed is an interesting metaphysical speculation. Does the pianist have to lay hold upon some Platonic form, some utterly abstract system of numerical relations, and, by the exercise of thought, imagination and will bring this down into the resonant medium of matter? Be that as it may, within the strictest limits of human life and action every performance, however good or bad, is once and for all. Performance is always unique. It is a moment of *living* appropriate to time, place and mood.

A moment of living. One feels that Emanuel Bach knew this well. Perhaps this is why he gives such a profuse and elaborate treatment of the whole question of ornamentation, for, in his view, no specific ornament should be finally reduced to a mere conventional formula. An ornament is part of the texture of a piece. Its expressive function and formal shape are largely determined by context – even the dynamics of the particular instrument being played upon must be taken into account. From the standpoint of Bach, an ornament which is just a conventional twist is virtually useless. An ornament is *par excellence* a moment of musical experience, a vehicle of feeling, an element in an affectional whole. Appropriately, it must never be casually standardized, but individualized by the encompassing mood of the piece to which, indeed, it contributes vitality and significance by reciprocal interaction.[2]

The exhortation to play from the soul shows that Bach was no mere calculator of effects, even though effects have frequently to be determined in the service of *Affekte*. Heartfelt performance, performance which has its creative dynamic in the depths of the soul, is performance which reveals the unity of the creative urge in and through the variety of its manifestations. The soul, that which is produced by 'the alchemical wedding' of spirit and matter (an esoteric idea very prevalent in Bach's day and fostered by mystics like Karl von Eckartshausen and the legends surrounding the mysterious Comte de St Germaine) in the human organism is not a merely feeling entity. It brings together the force of feeling, passion and intellect, and in so far as we say a work of musical art, or its performance, are inspired, we mean that it is in-formed by a unified creative urge which creates a wholeness out of diverse interacting parts.

We do not know if Emanuel Bach ever dwelt upon thoughts of this kind. Possibly he did not; but they were in the intellectual atmosphere which subconsciously fed his aesthetic aspirations, and his remarks in the *Essay* go some way towards indicating them.

In the chapter on Performance, we can read the mature observations of a serious composer who has meditated upon the relationship between the thought which is musical composition and the reliving of that thought which is performance. Performance takes place in the region of physical space through which the creative individuality manifests itself to the outside world. It follows that there must be a direct link between the subjective content of performance, the moment of creative imagination, the moment of musical living and the pattern of kinetic responses which manifest through the spatial structure of the keyboard. Everything that happens on the keyboard must be, in some sense, a manifestation of a state of mind. Bach gives a clue to his innermost perception when he observes (p. 154) that 'attack and touch are one and the same thing'. One might add that attack is a mental factor, touch a physical one. Such a remark could only have been made by a man who has discovered that the force with which the hands address the keys should be wholly determined by the subjective tonal image of the music which the performer is creating in his mind. This observation, together with those previously noted, lends substance to the overall implication that the creative thought is the most vital and most immediate dynamic of the movements of the hands.[3]

Knowing Bach's skill in improvisation, we can be sure that a capacity for spontaneous thinking with the hands (which is generally a sign of inborn musical genius) was his to a remarkable degree, and that he applied this capacity not only in the art of improvisation and fantasia, but also in the performance of his sonatas. We have already seen that the sonata, in Bach's consciousness, seemed to be a world of dialectical relationships. It is reasonable to suppose that he relived this world inwardly during performance, and that his dynamics, ornamentation, rubato and so on were spontaneously rendered by his hands in response to the subjective experience. In which case, the element of rational calculation of effect might very well, in his case, have been below that which he urges upon others in the *Essay*. But if that is so, then the *Essay* is a true work of theory, in that it leads the reader onwards and upwards through rational directives and intellectual precepts to that high point of musical insight when intuition alone reveals the secret – the ultimate secret of performance.

I think it goes without saying that pianists brought up on a diet of Czerny exercises are very likely to miss the point of C. P. E. Bach's keyboard figuration. Velocity studies which command a wide reach of keyboard space are no preparation for introspective rhapsody where the hands move within a comparatively narrow range. Let us not forget that much of Emanuel's keyboard music unconsciously adapts itself to the spatial limitations of the clavichord. This is not by any means always a disadvantage, because it concentrates attention upon details of structure and texture which often reward close study.

Related to this is another and perhaps more important factor. The peculiar physical pressures and the special sensitivity of the clavichord are unknown to the pianist who has never played upon the instrument. To turn to the clavichord after years of pianoforte experience is to look inwards into the world of tone, and to rediscover the *raison d'être* of the world of tone within oneself. Conversely, after playing the clavichord, one returns to the piano with some new insights into the relations between head, heart and hands, or, to put it another way, between the inner world of feeling and one's neuro-muscular co-ordinations. Almost unconsciously, perhaps, the hands move on the keys of the piano with a new sense of contact. Despite the fact that the hand cannot affect the sounding tone of the pianoforte string once the keys are depressed, the fingers almost persuade one that it can. This, of course, is a fantasy; but it is no fantasy to suggest that the clavichordist has something to teach the pianist. Much of the disappointment experienced by pianists who try out a clavichord for the first time results from their own crude insensitivity, and total lack of insight into the nature of the instrument. It is possible to make impressive noises upon a piano when the intellectual and feeling content of one's performance are minimal. The true musician will never be deceived, of course. The important point is that the clavichord often reveals a pianist's deficiencies to himself!

The following exercise is very rewarding, and it can open up new insights into the artistic demands of keyboard performance. Play fairly rapid repetitions of a triad (say D–F sharp A) in triplet time without consciously attempting to give prominence to any one tone. Now pause for a moment, and decide that the hand, whilst continuing to play the complete chord, is going to give successive prominence to the tones A, F sharp and D, almost as if playing them in single tones as a triplet. To achieve this rapidly by some method of purely physical control is not easy, indeed, it is extremely difficult.

In fact, the knack is very easily acquired. One does it without trying to do it by any conscious physical determination. It is enough to think and feel the triplet buried in the complete chord, as a purely subjective emotional and mental process completely divorced from any physical preoccupations whatsoever. The hand is completely relaxed: the muscular tensions are looked after by the unconscious mind: the conscious mind is concerned solely with the musical effect. The same exercise may be practised upon a guitar, with beautiful and illuminating results.

Many insights follow from this simple experiment. Sight-reading is immeasurably enriched once conscious attention is completely liberated from physiological preoccupation. Not least, the subjective feel of the linear thrust of tone within a vertical complex opens new well-springs of sensitivity in the performance of repeated chords. Mental insight into hidden unities of tonal structure can be translated, through feeling, into tone.

Once the pianist has gained some practical experience in the art of playing with mind and heart alone, he is free to enlarge and develop his practical understanding of music. The point I wish to make is that the clavichord is, in fact, an instrument which opens up this kind of intuition. It invites the performer to play with his heart and mind, from the soul, as Bach would say, and not like a trained bird — or, one might add, like a typist or sewing-machine operator. The technique of the clavichord almost compels an introspective self-communing, and virtually insists that tone is feeling before it is anything else.

The plangent sounds with which Emanuel Bach delighted Dr Burney can never be successfully imitated upon a modern piano. Even so, some proficiency in the exercise described above may enable the pianist to achieve an approximate *Bebung* effect. On a clavichord, successive stabs of feeling on a single tone, indicated in the notation by a slur and a series of dots, can become an almost instinctive response to subjective emotional evocation. Similarly, in the performance of repeated chords, which should emphatically not be regarded as colourless repetitions to be casually tapped out by the hand, the repetitions may be grouped as momentary throbs within a single impulsion. This, in my opinion, is how the right-hand chords should be regarded in the first few bars of the beautiful Fantasia in F sharp minor entitled *C. P. E. Bachs Empfindungen*. Having played this piece upon a clavichord, one tends to approach the slow movement of Beethoven's Sonata in A flat, opus 110 with new insights. It is expecially interesting that Beethoven, in the opening recitative of this movement, composes an imitative *Bebung*. Here we see a reappraisal, in terms of pianoforte technique, of the expressive idiom of the clavichord.

When experimenting with such effects upon the piano keyboard, the hand, wrist and arm must be completely relaxed. The effect to be achieved must be considered from a completely subjective standpoint. All the music, so to speak, must be in the heart. The hands, and the keyboard, will look after themselves. It is an undoubted fact that the sensitivity of one's neuro-muscular co-ordinations, one's capacity, that is, to react instantaneously to the directives of pure feeling willed into objectivity, is greatest when the body is relaxed and when the mind is withdrawn from physiological preoccupation. Granting such a condition of relaxation – which is a far more profound state than that consciously produced by Matthay exercises – it is only necessary to sanction the impulses of musical thought and feeling. Close observation of the hand and arm – as if they belonged to someone else – will reveal that the tonal impulse flicks down the forearm, hand and into the fingers like an electric shock. The speed of the flicks will depend upon the tonal quality of the musical impulsion. As on feels, so will the hand react.

On a clavichord, the hands will not leave the keys. On a piano, the pressure of the fingers will be alternately relaxed and intensified sufficiently to permit the keys to be raised and depressed slightly. Naturally, everything will depend upon the quality of the instrument and the insight gained by the performer. A bad instrument which will not permit the rapid repetition of notes, is useless for this kind of experiment. A good instrument is equally useless if the performer cannot appreciate the fact that the mind and heart alone will look after all the technical aspects of performance. To simplify a complex psycho-physical phenomenon, one might say that the conscious mind (head) works through the soul (heart–feeling) to stimulate the unconscious neuro-muscular co-ordinations of the arm, wrist and hand.

I am personally convinced that Emanuel Bach knew a good deal about this, and that all his practice devoted to the achievement of a singing tone was motivated by his experience of the technique of the clavichord in association with the aesthetic of *Empfindsamkeit*. If we are to understand his music and play it intelligently, it is worth giving some thought to the psychological basis of the technique which underlies it.

Three Fugues

Fugue in D minor

C. P. E. Bach
1758 Wotquenne 119/2

Fugue in A

C. P. E. Bach
1757 Wotquenne 119/4

Fugue in E flat

C. P. E. Bach
1762 Wotquenne 119/6

Notes

Chapter one

[1] For an English translation see *Letters of Distinguished Musicians*, ed. Lady G. M. Wallace, London, 1857–9. The German original, together with other interesting autobiographical material by Hässler, Quantz and others may be seen in *Selbstbiographien deutscher Musiker des XVIII Jahrhunderts*, ed. Willi Kahl, Hinrichsen, 1948.

[2] See: F. W. Marpurg, *Der critische Musicus an der Spree*, 1749–50
J. F. Agricola, *Anleitung zur Singkunst*, 1757
C. G. Krause, *Von der musicalischen Poesie*, 1752
J. J. Quantz, *Versuch einer Anweisung die Flöte traversiere zu spielen*, 1752
J. G. Sulzer, *Pensées sur l'origine et les différents emplois des sciences et des beaux-arts*, 1757
J. P. Kirnberger, *Konstruktion der gleichschwebenden Temperatur*, 1760
Die Kunst des reinen Satzes, 1774–9.

[3] The reader's attention is also drawn to the fine Cello Concerto in A, DGG recording LPM 18816.

Chapter two

[1] Peter Pirie in a review of Arthur Hutchings's 'The Invention and composition of Music', *Music Review*, Vol. XXI/4, p. 335.

[2] It has been suggested that Berlioz was fascinated by the visual aspect of harmonic configurations in notation. See Philip Friedheim: 'Radical harmonic procedures in Berlioz', *Music Review*, Vol. XXI/4, pp. 282–96. See also my analysis of C. P. E. Bach's Rondo in A minor in Chapter twelve.

[3] I have suggested elsewhere that as Hegel is to philosophy, so is Beethoven to music. See my articles: 'Beethoven und Hegel', *Musica heft* 10, 1953, pp. 437–40, and 'The Sonata-principle: a study of musical thought in the eighteenth century', *Music Review*, Vol. XIII, 1952, pp. 255–63.

[4] Teilhard de Chardin: *The Phenomenon of Man*. The 'omega point' is the summit and end of the evolutionary process conceived not only as a physical movement but also as mental and spiritual. The idea is that the end of all will be the comprehension of all. In relation to such a final and ultimate viewpoint, all individual viewpoints must be partitive and relative. Unfortunately, the human conception of an hypothetical omega point must also seem partitive and subject to the same principle of relativity. Nevertheless, the belief that some ultimate supra-personal insight

into the total scheme of things is an eventual possibility for spiritually evolved human nature has obstinately reappeared in every age of philosophy, even as it has in our own day. The historian, at any rate, and especially the historian of art, can never escape the relativity of his judgements. He can, however, refuse to limit himself by merely outward appearances. Empiricism in musicology is an absurd restriction of the critical faculty and can lead to nothing but fragmentation and sterile analysis. The study of a period through the analysis of musical scores must be furthered by the exercise of historical imagination in more than notational matters, and some appeal to intuition.

5 'Three intellectual operations; three terms in the syllogism; three figures in argument; three intrinsic principles in natural things . . . three lines in the whole universe.' See O. Strunk: *Source Readings in Musical History*. A more recent enthusiast for the number three was Hugo Riemann who went to great pains in his editions of the classics to demonstrate that all musical forms and rhythmic structures were dominated by the principle of triplicity.

6 I accept the Jungian analysis of the unconscious mind in its general outlines; but I would carry it somewhat farther in defining the nature of the universal forces which flow through the collective unconscious, up into the individual unconscious and finally through to consciousness. The main point here is that whereas empirical musicology must confine itself to chronological manifestations of a trend, a more penetrating insight will support the idea that temporal manifestation in consciousness may well be an erratic, spasmodic and not necessarily orderly unfolding of something already complete in the collective unconscious. One might very well, for instance, discover examples of a specific musical form before the trend of which it is a manifestation has worked itself up into a definitive conscious expression. Taking this a stage farther, we have to reckon with the idea that all musical forms, and even the root intervallic relationships from which music grows, are manifestations of the structure of human thought when projected into tone. It would then follow that any musicological investigation of the history of a particular form or style would be tantamount to an investigation of the universal mentalism of consciousness – an inquiry into the nature of the 'self'. See my article: 'History and Theory in Musical Appreciation', *Musical Opinion*, Vol. LXXXII, pp. 163–5; also Lazare Saminsky: *Physics and Metaphysics of Music*, Nijhoff, The Hague, 1957, and my review of this book in *Music Review*, August 1958.

7 See 'History and Theory in Musical Appreciation', and my paper: 'The Thought in Musical History', *Monthly Musical Record*, Vol. LXXXIII, 1953, pp. 200–8.

8 See George Lesser: *Gothic Cathedrals and Sacred Geometry*, two vols., Tiranti, 1957: also my article 'The Concept of Bach', *Music Review*, Vol. XXIII, 1962, pp. 261–70.

9 For Herbert Read a work of art is 'a pattern informed by sensibility'.

10 This implication is negative in that it is retrospective, and positive in that it is prospective. In relation to the climactic point of present, heard sound, the past remembered context is a fixed determinant, whereas the future, anticipated context is still uncertain although subject to eventual

determination by the present. When the last chord is sounded, the total formal context is negative and fixed, an established objective fact. We can see how creation is thus the negation of a positive impulse, the objective fixing or capture of a subjective drive, the 'death' of energy in form. Music is a particular case, giving a potent analogy, of a universal process in the creative consciousness.

[11] See my article: 'Philosophical Problems in Musical Criticism', *Music Review*, February 1964, Vol. XXV, pp. 1–16.

Chapter three

[1] The most recent classification appears to be that of Paz Corazon G. Canave in *A re-evaluation of the role played by Carl Philip Emanuel Bach in the development of the Clavier Sonata*, Catholic University of America Press, 1956.

[2] I have examined many keyboard works by Bach's contemporaries. Two things stand out: (*a*) Italianate tunefulness together with somewhat stereotyped accompaniments, Alberti-fashion, (*b*) imitation of C. P. E. Bach's style – especially in the slow movements. An apparent anxiety to shy away from contrapuntal methods leads to thin two-part writing, of which Bach himself was often guilty. Fugue, on the other hand, becomes academically self-conscious. Friedman Bach, G. Benda, Neefe and Fasch embraced Emanuel Bach's aesthetic but did not follow it so consistently. In their best work they achieved some interesting music which will stand comparison with Bach's. Neefe was a special admirer of Emanuel Bach and leaned heavily upon Bach's *Essay on the True Art of Playing Keyboard Instruments*.

[3] The main sources are:

(*a*) Gottlieb Friedrich Schrieben: *Verzeichniss des Nachlasses der verstorben Capellmeisters C. P. E. Bach*, 1790. The dates in this catalogue are those inscribed by Bach himself upon his own manuscripts.

(*b*) Carl Hermann Bitter compiled a catalogue from Schrieber's list in 1868. See *Carl Philipp Emanuel und Wilhelm Friedmann Bach und deren Bruder*, 2 vols, Berlin, 1868.

(*c*) Alfred Wotquenne: *Catalogue thématique des oeuvres de Charles Philippe Emmanuel Bach*, Leipzig, 1905. Wotquenne made his catalogue at Brussels where there is a big collection of C. P. E. Bach's music. Another collection is held at the library of the Paris Conservatoire. Paz Corazon G. Canave has done useful work in listing the various collections throughout which Emanuel's sonatas are scattered.

[4] See my article: 'Some after-thoughts of C. P. E. Bach, *Monthly Musical Record*, Vol. XC, pp. 94–98. The alterations were made in 1788, according to the date inscribed by Bach on the printed copy.

Chapter four

[1] Charles Burney: *The Present State of Music in Germany, the Netherlands and United Provinces*, London, 1773.

² D. Suzuki: 'From Zen to the Gandavyuha' in *Essays on Zen Buddhism*, 3rd series, Rider.

³ It might be better to describe chess as dynamic relationship at once objectively contemplated and subjectively felt. In this sense it is not unlike music. Part of the fascination of chess derives from the fact that objective patterns do have a kind of subjective *nisus* – in other words, one can imaginatively dramatize a situation by projecting oneself into it. On the other hand, the consistent winner is the man who can resist such a *nisus* and keep a cool head. It is possible that skill in improvisation depends upon the speed with which the musician can thrust the subjective upsurge into objectivity where he can, so to speak, *see* it.

⁴ *Essay*, Part II, Chapter 7, v. p. 431, in Mitchell's translation (1951).

⁵ The term 'musical time-space' requires a little elucidation here, although the idea it embodies is developed later on (see Chapter seven). Ordinary day-to-day experience is bounded by our subjective relationship with the spread of events in time and the spatial continuum of our visual perceptions and physical movements. In listening to music we voluntarily withdraw attention from the environment in general, closing down our visual perceptions and retaining the primary element of *time*. The performer, of course, fuses movement in space, vision, hearing and temporal relationship in the re-creative act. The main point, however, is that as far as the end-result of performance is concerned, time in general is 'framed' or ordered by musical time, and our world of spatial apprehension is reduced to the single dimension of tone, within which our thoughts and emotions 'move'. Pure concentration upon the tonal essence is for most listeners an impossible ideal. In some cases it is not even desirable – especially when the avowed intent is to arouse emotion or to express ideas. However, assuming time and tone to be the primary ingredients of music, we can analogously regard melody as the time-element and harmony as the space-element in the musician's world. In the traditional system of Western harmony, the archetypal formative principle of tonal space is the triad. From the relationships contained in this chord, all others can be derived, and they include the definitive order of harmonic relations and of melody. A composer orders his material within two dimensions, with an alternating tendency of emphasis to one or the other, or with a perpetual balance between the two. I would suggest that in the idiom of Bach and Handel we can contemplate continuous balance; whereas in the reactionary phase prior to the consolidation of the Viennese aesthetic, harmony and melody are alternately overthrowing one another. This condition of instability in the time-space of music is correlative with the aesthetic of *Empfindsamkeit* and *Sturm und Drang*. The history of music constantly reveals a dislocation of the equilibrium between the alternating polarities of melody and harmony. It is especially interesting that the 'humanization' of music in the sixteenth century gradually brought to the fore a preoccupation with harmony, the space-element of music, whereas objectification and intellectualism generally find expression in melodic abstraction and contrapuntal mathematics. It is as if pure tonal space is correlative with pure subjectivity and space, and melody, in order to exist at all, always introduces an objective element of shape through the arrangement of a temporal series. To carry this speculation back to its

implicit first principles: if the universe consisted only of pure space, the correlative consciousness could only be a feeling-state of pure beingness devoid of form. If, on the other hand, the universe were purely linear (which is logically impossible because the concept of linear relation pre-supposes the concept of space) the correlative consciousness could only be a state of abstract thought devoid of feeling. Music as we understand it could not exist in either kind of universe. The experience of music is an experience of relationships which can only exist in the temporal organiza-tion of a subjectively idealized tonal space. The true medium of music is the medium of physical space-time elevated to the status of an ideal concept in which the polarized opposites of subject and object are over-come. In other words a musical relation is a relation which is not only heard, but thought and felt.

[6] Bernard Bosanquet: *History of Aesthetic*, Chapter 9, Section 3/vi.

[7] Op. cit., Chapter 4, Section 6/a–iv.

[8] Op. cit., Chapter 4, Section 6/a–iv.

[9] There is a recording of this work played on the clavichord in the *H.M.V. History of Music in Sound*, Vol. vii, *The Symphonic Outlook*, ed. Gerald Abraham.

[10] See H. Schenker: 'Die Kunst der Improvisation' in *Das Meisterwerk in der Musik*, Vol. 1, Munich, 1925.
Also H. Schenker: *Neue Musikalische Theorien und Phantasien Harmonielehre, Kontrapunkt, Der Freie Satz*, Universal Edition, Wien.

[11] Adele Katz: *Challenge to Musical Tradition*, U.S.A., 1945.

[12] Marius Schneider: 'Primitive Music', Chapter I, in *The New Oxford History of Music*, Vol. I.

[13] Gustave Reese: *Music in the Middle Ages*, Chapter VI, Dent, 1941.

[14] See 'A Fantasia by C. P. E. Bach', *Monthly Musical Record*, Vol. LXXXV, 1955, pp. 144–50.

Chapter five

[1] As I see it, the emergence of a new musical style, the extension of existing forms, the development of harmony and so on – all these are the ex-pressions of a new manner of experiencing, not simply causes of it. The outer manifestations of form and style are the correlatives of an inner growth, the objective counterpole of a subjective vitality. A new phase of consciousness has its leading representatives, of course, and their work certainly influences and provokes subjective growth in their cultural environment; but a truer insight is that an innovator is the first upthrust of new subjective pressures stirring in the collective mind.

Chapter six

[1] For example, Davison and Apel, in the second volume of their *Historical Anthology of Music*, quote a symphonic movement of J. T. Monn dating from 1740 which is a complete example of sonata-form.

² Beethoven, like Haydn, admired C. P. E. Bach's sonatas, although he probably did not have such an intimate knowledge of them as Haydn who played them by the hour in his earlier days. Beethoven himself made copies of the fourth and fifth 'Württemberg' sonatas, and his teacher, Neefe, according to Thayer, was 'a devout student of them'.

³ See Basil Willey: 'Essay on Coleridge' in *Nineteenth Century Studies*, Chatto and Windus, 1949.

⁴ We find such a tendency, for example, in the tropes and sequences of the Middle Ages, in the technique of theme and variations, in every phase of the evolution of the sonata, in the song-like forms of the nineteenth century and so on.

⁵ There are certain obvious exceptions to this generalization – as, for instance, in the case of the strophic *Lied*.

⁶ Analyzed at length by D. F. Tovey in his volume on *Chamber Music*.

⁷ C. P. E. Bach's north German contemporaries (see Note 2, Chapter three) were strongly influenced by the cult of *Empfindsamkeit*; but although they appeared to imitate Bach in their adoption of the new style, they did not really grasp the principle of synthesis, the unification of the new emotional dynamic with the extended binary conception (which they all seemed to accept without question) with the same musical penetration displayed by Bach.

Chapter seven

¹ Consider this stimulating passage from S. Alexander's *Artistic Creation and Cosmic Creation*: 'As the work of art is the fusion of spirit and matter in finite ingredients, so within this space-time which is below fusion, there is an element which corresponds to spirit and one which corresponds to matter, and these are respectively time and space. Time is, as it were, the mind to the body which is space. . . . In spirit and body as we know them, whether in organism or in the new creation by man which art supplies, spirit is the time and body or material the space element in these highly developed creations of the world process. Our life is the time of our body, which is the space of our life. . . .'

² See my paper: 'The Concept of Bach', *Music Review*, Vol. XXIII, 1962, pp. 261–70.

³ Hegel: *Introduction to the Philosophy of Fine Art* (Bosanquet's translation), Kegan Paul, 1905. 'The . . . art in which the romantic type realizes itself is contrasted with painting, and is music. Its medium, though still sensuous, yet develops into still more thorough subjectivity and particularization. Music . . . treats the sensuous as ideal, and does so by negating, and idealizing into the individual isolation of a single point, the indifferent externality of space. . . .' Bosanquet comments on this: 'The negation of space is an attribute of music. The parts of a chord are no more in space than are the parts of a judgement. Hegel expresses this by saying that music idealizes space and concentrates it into a point.'

⁴ A not entirely irrelevant quotation springs to mind: 'Give me *extension*,' said Descartes, 'and I will make a world'. To Gustav Mahler a symphony was explicitly a world. He was an expert in the art of extending vertical

relations, as his use of the interval of the fourth in the first symphony reveals. The thematic archetype used by Mahler in almost everything of significance which he wrote, is also revealed in its simplest forms as an extension of the chord of the added sixth. See my article: 'Mahler – a thematic archetype', *Music Review*, Vol. XXI, 1960, pp. 297–316. The image of a musical structure being a *world* is quite logically suggested by Emanuel Bach's conception of the sonata-principle.
5 See 'The Concept of Bach' (ref. above, Note 2).

Chapter eight

1 Edward Caird: 'Goethe and Philosophy' – in *Essays in Literature and Philosophy*, Vol. I, Glasgow, 1892.
2 Op. cit.
3 See the Sonata in B minor Opus 40 No 2. There is a recording of part of Clementi's sonata in *H.M.V. History of Music in Sound*, Vol. VIII, Side V, Band 2.

Chapter nine

1 J. S. Shedlock: *The Pianoforte Sonata*, Methuen, 1895.

Chapter eleven

1 It is interesting to compare the dates:

C. P. E. Bach	1714–1788
Beethoven	1770–1827
Hegel	1770–1831
Goethe	1749–1832
Schelling	1775–1854
Fichte	1762–1814.

Chapter twelve

(1) For a clavichord recording see *Archiv* 37 120 EPA.

Chapter thirteen

1 Karl Geiringer: *The Bach Family*, Allen and Unwin, 1954.
2 They were published in a number of collections:
Geistliche Lieder und Oden 1758 and 1764
Psalmen mit Melodien 1774
Geistliche Gesänge mit Melodien zum Singen bei dem Claviere 1780–1
Neue Lieder melodien (post.) 1789.

Chapter fourteen

1 C. F. Cramer: *Magazin der Musik*, 1786.
2 He sold the engraved plates for the price of the metal.

Appendix one

1 The references in the text are to the 1951 edition of W. J. Mitchell's translation of the *Versuch*.
2 On the whole matter of ornamentation in C. P. E. Bach's keyboard music the best authority is the composer himself. See the *Versuch*, Chapter II, Part 1. Schott's editions of the *Probe-Stücke* and the fantasia *C. P. E. Bachs Empfindungen* are supplied with a useful introduction to the subject.
3 The keyboard performer interested in the systematic development of this idea should study Luigi Bonpensiere: *New Pathways to Piano Technique*. A study of the relations between Mind and Body with special reference to piano-playing. Philosophical Library, New York, 1953. See also my review article: 'Mind, Hands and Keyboard', *Music and Letters*, Vol. XXXVI, 1955, pp. 226–32.

Bibliography

BACH, C. P. E.: *Versuch über die wahre Art das Clavier zu spielen*, Berlin, 1759, 1762. Reprint by Walter Niemann, fifth edition, Leipzig, 1925. Translated into English by William J. Mitchell, New York, 1949. Published in Great Britain 1949. Second edition 1951 (Cassell).

BARFORD, P. T.: 'The Sonata Principle; a Study of Musical Thought in the Eighteenth Century', *Music Review*, XIII (Nov. 1952), pp. 254–63.

—— *Beethoven und Hegel*, trans. Karl H. Wörner, Musica 1953/Heft 10, pp. 437–40.

—— 'A Fantasia by C. P. E. Bach', *Monthly Musical Record*, Vol. 85, pp. 144–50.

—— 'Some Afterthoughts by C. P. E. Bach', *Monthly Musical Record*, Vol. 90, pp. 94–98.

BITTER, C. H.: *C. P. E. und W. F. Bach und deren Brüder*, Berlin, 1868.

BOSANQUET, B.: *History of Aesthetic*, G. A. and Unwin, 1892.

BURNEY, CH.: *The Present State of Music in Germany, the Netherlands and United Provinces*, London, 1773.

CAIRD, E.: *Essays on Literature and Philosophy*, Vols. I and II, Glasgow, 1892.

CANAVE, P. C. G.: *A Re-Evaluation of the Role Played by Carl Philipp Emanuel Bach in the Development of the Clavier Sonata*, Catholic University of America Press, Washington D.C., 1956.

CHERBULIEZ, A. E.: *Carl Philip Emanuel Bach*, Zürich, 1940.

CHRYSANDER, F.: 'Eine Klavierphantasie von Karl Philipp Emanuel Bach', *Vierteljahrschrift für Musikwissenschaft*, No. 7, 1891.

CLERCX, S.: 'La forme du Rondo chez Carl Philipp Emanuel Bach', *Revue de Musicologie*, Vol. XVI, pp. 148ff., Paris, 1935.

CRAMER, C. F. (editor): *Magazin der Musik*, Jg. 1–2, Hamburg, 1783–7, and Jg. 3, Copenhagen, 1789.

GEIRINGER, K.: *The Bach Family – Seven Generations of Creative Genius*, G. A. and Unwin, 1954.

HEGEL, F.: *Aesthetik. Introduction to the Philosophy of Fine Art*, translated, with an introductory essay by B. Bosanquet, London, 1905.

MIESNER, H.: *Philipp Emanuel Bach in Hamburg*, Leipzig, 1929.

NEWMAN, W. S.: *The Keyboard Sonatas of Bach's Sons*, Proceedings of Music Teachers National Association, Pittsburgh, Pa., 1951.

NOHL, L.: *Letters of Distinguished Musicians* (containing C. P. E. Bach's autobiography and ten letters), translated from the German by Lady Wallace, London, Longmans, Green & Co., 1867.

PLAMENAC, D.: 'New Light on the Last Years of Carl Philipp Emanuel Bach', *Musical Quarterly*, 1949.

REESER, E.: *The Sons of Bach*, Symphonia Books, The Continental Book Co A. B. Stockholm (no date).

RIEMANN, H.: 'Die Söhne Bachs', *Präludien und Studien*, Vol. III, Leipzig, 1901.

SCHEIBE, J. A.: *Critischer Musicus*, Leipzig, 1745.

SCHENKER, H.: 'Die Kunst der Improvisation', *Das Meisterwerk in der Musik*, Vol. I, Munich, 1925.

—— *Ein Beitrag zur Ornamentik*, Universal Edition, 1908.

—— *Der Tonwille*, series of analytical pamphlets published Vienna, 1921–3.

SCHERING, A.: 'Carl Philipp Emanuel Bach und das "redende Prinzip" in der Musik', *Jahrbuch der Musikbibliothek Peters*, Vol. 45, 1938.

SCHMID, E. F.: 'Haydn und Ph. Em. Bach', *Zeitschrift für Musikwissenschaft*, XIV, pp. 299ff., 1931–2.

SHEDLOCK, J. S.: *The Pianoforte Sonata – Its Origin and Development*, Methuen, 1895. (This book contains one of the earliest scholarly assessments of C. P. E. Bach's keyboard sonatas in English.)

VRIESLANDER, O.: 'Carl Philipp Emanuel Bach als Theoretiker', *Von neuer Musik*, Cologne, 1925.
—— *Carl Philipp Emanuel Bach*, Munich, 1923.
WOTQUENNE, A.: *Catalogue thématique des oeuvres de Charles Philippe Emmanuel Bach*, Leipzig, 1905.
—— *Thematisches Verzeichnis der Werke von C. Ph. E. Bach*, reprint of the 1905 edition, Breitkopf & Hartel, 1964.

Discography of Keyboard Works of C. P. E. Bach

Note: Only long-playing records have been included: those interested in 78 r.p.m. recordings are referred to *World's Encyclopaedia of Recorded Music* by Clough and Cumming and to relevant catalogues. All records are 12 in. except where stated: numbers in italics indicate 7 in. extended-play records. Most records listed, except those marked (*d*), which are deleted, can now be obtained in this country either from specialist dealers or by direct importation from the country of origin. This is indicated by initials in brackets following the catalogue number, viz: (A) Austria; (F) France; (G) Germany (Federal Republic); (H) Hungary; (US) United States.

Kenneth Dommett
Birmingham 1965

W.33	Sonata in A minor
	Hugo Ruf (cembalo), Bärenreiter BM 30 L 1520 (m) (G)
W.55/4	Sonata in A
	Nina Milkina (piano), Westminster XWN 18853 (US) (*d*)
W.56/5–6	Sonata and Rondo No. 3 in A
	Fritz Neumeyer (clavichord), Archive *epa 37120*
W.57/1	Sonata in A minor
W.57/3	Sonata in F minor
	Nina Milkina (piano), Westminster XWN 18853 (US) (*d*)
W.57/4	Sonata in D minor
	Dorothy Eustis (piano), Artist 501 (US) (*d*)
W.59/1	Sonata in E minor
W.59/2	Rondo in G
	Ruggiero Gerlin (harpsichord), Oiseau-Lyre OL 50097 (*d*)
W.59/6	Fantasia in C
	Herman Iseringhausen (clavichord), Cantate *643302*
W.61/1	Sonata in D
	Nina Milkina (piano), Westminster XWN 18853 (US) (*d*)
W.63/6–III	Fantasia in C minor
	Dorothy Swainson (clavichord), HMV HLP 19; Victor LM–6137 (US)
W.63/1–6	Six 'Essay' Sonatas (*Probe-Stücke*)
	Elisabeth Katzenellenbogen
	(1790, Broadwood piano), Lyrichord LL 63 (US)
W.65/31	Sonata in C minor
(in W.266)	Dorel Handman (piano), Oiseau-Lyre OL 50078 (*d*)
W.70/6	Sonata in G minor
	Anthon van der Horst (chamber organ), Telefunken AWT 9447C (m), SAWT 9447B (s)
W.117/2	Solfeggietto in C minor
	member of Collegium Pro Arte (harpsichord), Oiseau-Lyre OL 50017
W.117/2	Solfeggietto in C minor (arr. Gilman)
	Hubert Jelinek (harp), Amadeo AVRS 6230 (A)
W.117/13	Chromatic fantasia
	Daniel Pinkham (harpsichord), Lyrichord LL 57 (US)
W.119/7	Fantasia and fugue in C minor
	Piet Kee (organ), Telefunken AWT 9447C (m), SAWT 944B (s)

Unidentified keyboard works

Fantasia in F sharp minor
? Benson (clavichord), Repertoire 901 (US)
Rondo in C minor

Maria Kalamkarian (clavier), Columbia C.70482 (G)
Sonata No. 2 in F
Jozsef Gàt (clavichord), Qualiton LPX 1151 (H)

Unidentified sonatas
John Newmark (Clementi piano), Folkways 3341 (US)

Twelve variations on *Folies d'Espagne*
John Newmark (fortepiano), Newmark RS 4 (Canada)

Modern editions of C. P. E. Bach's solo keyboard music

Edition Schott

2353   *Sechs Sonaten* (Volume I, Sonatas 1–3.)

2354   *Sechs Sonaten* (Volume II, Sonatas 4–6, Fantasia in C minor.)
         Achtzehn Probe-Stücke zu dem Versuch über die wahre Art das Clavier zu
         spielen (1753) (Wotquenne 63).   ·

2826   *Zwei Sonaten für Klavier*
         Sonata in F, Leipzig, 1734. Berlin, 1744 (Wotquenne 64/1). (The first of a
         set of six keyboard sonatinas.)
         Sonata in E flat (no Wotquenne classification).

4013   *Zwei Klavierstücke*
         Fantasia in F sharp minor. *C. P. E. Bachs Empfindungen*, Hamburg, 1787
         (Wotquenne 67).
         Rondo in E minor. *Abschied vom Silbermannschen Clavier*, Hamburg, 1781
         (Wotquenne 66).

F.S.30   Presto

07966   *Solfeggietto*

1519   'Sons of Bach' Album of thirteen original pieces.

4747   *Leichte Klavierstücke der Vorklassik*
         Easy piano pieces from the sons of Bach to Beethoven.

3975   '15 Sonatas of the Pre-Classical Period'
         Sonatas by C. P. E. Bach, Hassler, Hasse, Kuhnau, Mehul, etc.

Keith Prowse & Co Ltd

Allemande in E Minor (arr. by Ernest Haywood) Berlin 1751 (Wotquenne 61/12). Part
         of a suite in five movements.

J. & W. Chester

Chester Library 74 and 75

'Eighteenth Century Music', Vols. I and II. Volume I contains four pieces by C. P. E.
         Bach, and Volume II six pieces. All are light and easy compositions. Some
         of the pieces in this collection are from *Kurze und liechte Stücke*. See Universal
         Edition 13311.

Nordiska Musikförlaget

Edition Musicalia No. 114

Sonata in C minor. Berlin 1957 (Wotquenne 65/31). This is a fine composition in the
         composer's maturest keyboard style. The thematic content is intrinsically
         interesting and well worked out. It stands up to performance on a modern
         piano, and has been competently edited by Karl Wohlfart.

Mitteldeutscher Verlag

Sechs Sonaten für das Klavier. This set appeared first in 1773 under the title: *Sei Sonate
         per il Clavicembalo solo all'uso delle Donne, composte da Carlo Filippo Emanuele
         Bach, Maestro di Capella in Hamburgo* (Wotquenne number 54). The sonatas
         are easy but attractive works.

Universal Edition

548a   *Klavierwerke.* Critical Edition by Heinrich Schenker. These volumes contain

548b   pieces from the collections for connoisseurs and amateurs.

11015   *Clavierstücke.* Contains minuets, characteristic pieces and other simple com-
         positions. This album, together with Chester Library 74/75, gives a good
         selection of C. P. E. Bach's lighter pieces.

13311   (Wiener Urtext Ausgabe)

Kurze und leichte Stücke mit veränderten Reprisen. Berlin, 1766 and 1768 (Wotquenne 113 and 114). A critical editorial report is separately available for this collection.

10787   'The Bach Family'. Compositions by twelve Bachs.

Nagel Edition
Nagels Musik-Archiv
NMA 65 'Short Pieces for Piano'.
NMA 90 'Easy Sonatas'.
NMA 6 'Prussian' Sonatas Book I (Wotquenne 48). 1/3.
NMA 15 'Prussian' Sonatas Book II. 4/6.
NMA 21 'Württemberg' Sonatas Book I (Wotquenne 49). 1/3.
NMA 22 'Württemberg' Sonatas Book II. 4/6.

British and Continental Music Agencies Ltd. (Agent for Breitkopf and Hartel)
Die sechs Sammlungen von Sonaten, Freien Fantasien und Rondos für Kenner und Liebhaber
Erste Sammlung. Sechs Clavier-Sonaten.
Zweite Sammlung. Clavier-Sonaten nebst einigen Rondos fürs Forte-Piano.
Dritte Sammlung. Clavier-Sonaten nebst einigen Rondos fürs Forte-Piano.
Vierte Sammlung. Clavier-Sonaten und Freie Fantasien nebst einigen Rondos fürs Forte-Piano.
Fünfte Sammlung. Clavier-Sonaten und Freie Fantasien nebst einigen Rondos fürs Forte-Piano.
Sechste Sammlung. Clavier-Sonaten und Freie Fantasien nebst einigen Rondos fürs Forte-Piano.
         (Wotquenne numbers 55, 56, 57, 58, 59 and 61 respectively.)

Peters Edition
H-8   'Bach's Sons'
        Twelve pieces by C. P. E., J. C., J. Christoph, W. F. Bach.
P-4188 'C. P. E. Bach: 4 Sonatas, 12 variations, etc.'
        This useful little collection includes the following sonatas:
        Sonata in C minor No. 3 of *Fortsetzung von sechs Sonaten* (Wotquenne 51).
        Sonata in G major (Wotquenne 65/48). Hamburg, 1783.
        Sonata in G minor No. 3 of *Zweite Fortsetzung von sechs Sonaten* (Wotquenne 52).
        Sonata in B flat No. 5 of *Sechs Sonaten für Clavier mit veränderten Reprisen* (Wotquenne 50).
P-276   'C. P. E. Bach: 6 Sonatas' edited by Hans von Bülow in 1862.
        Of this edition, J. S. Shedlock in his book *The Pianoforte Sonata* (1895) made the following comment:
        'The late Dr. Bülow edited six of Emanuel Bach's sonatas, and though he
        was well acquainted with the composer's style of writing, his anxious
        desire to present the music in the most favourable light sometimes led him
        to make changes of which even lenient judges would not approve.'
        The sonatas in this collection are:
No. 1. Sonata in F minor. No. 3 in the third volume for Connoisseurs and Amateurs.
    2. Sonata in A minor. No. 1 in the third volume for Connoisseurs and Amateurs.
    3. Sonata in A major. No. 4 in the first collection for Connoisseurs and Amateurs.
    4. Sonata in G major. No. 6 in the same collection.
    5. Sonata in D minor. No. 2 in the third volume for Connoisseurs and Amateurs.
    6. Sonata in A flat. No. 2 of the Württemberg set.

Index